FOOD FOR THOUGHT

Food for Thought
Towards a Future
for Farming

PATRICK HERMAN AND RICHARD KUPER FOR THE
CONFÉDÉRATION PAYSANNE

Pluto Press
London • Sterling, Virginia

This book is based on *Changeons de politique agricole*, produced for the Confédération Paysanne by Patrick Herman and published in 2002 by Mille et une nuits, an imprint of Arthème Fayard, Paris. It has been translated into English, adapted and updated by Richard Kuper, in close consultation with Jean Damien Terreaux of the Confédération.

First published 2002 by Mille et une nuits, an imprint of Arthème Fayard, Paris.

English translation published 2003 by Pluto Press 345 Archway Road, London N6 5AA and 22883 Quicksilver Drive, Sterling, VA 20166-2012, USA

www.plutobooks.com

British Library Cataloguing in Publication Data
A catalogue record for this book is available from the British Library

Library of Congress Cataloging-in-Publication Data

Herman, Patrick.
Food for thought: towards a future for farming /
Patrick Herman and Richard Kuper.
p. cm.
Includes bibliographical references.
ISBN 0–7453–2078–3 (hbk) – ISBN 0–7453–2077–5 (pbk)
1. Agriculture and state–European Union countries. 2. Agriculture and state–France. 3. Confédération paysanne. 4. Produce trade–Government policy–European Union countries. 5. Produce trade–Government policy–France. I. Kuper, Richard. II. Title.
HD1918.H47 2003
338.1'844–dc22
2003017306

10 9 8 7 6 5 4 3 2 1

ISBN 0 7453 2078 3 hardback
ISBN 0 7453 2077 5 paperback

Designed and produced for Pluto Press by
Curran Publishing Services, Norwich

Printed and bound in the European Union by
Antony Rowe Ltd, Chippenham and Eastbourne, England

Contents

Boxes

Abbreviations

ACP African, Caribbean and Pacific group of states

AoA Agreement on Agriculture of the Uruguay Round

ATTAC Association pour la taxation des transactions financières pour l'aide aux citoyens (literally: Association for the Taxation of Financial Transactions to Aid Citizens; ATTAC International describes itself as an international movement for democratic control of financial markets and their institutions)

CAP Common Agricultural Policy

CEECs Central and Eastern European Countries

CITES Convention on International Trade in Endangered Species of Wild Fauna and Flora

CNJA Centre nationale des jeunes agriculteurs (National Centre for Young Farmers) (CDJA refers to departmental groupings of the CNJA)

CNSTP Confédération national des syndicates de travailleurs paysans (National Confederation of Unions of Worker Farmers)

COGECA Comité générale de la coopération agricole de l'Union Européenne (General Committee for Agricultural Cooperation in the European Union)

COPA Comité des organisations professionnelles agricoles de l'Union Européenne (Committee of Agricultural Organisations in the European Union)

CPE Coordination Paysanne Européenne (European Farmers Coordination)

EEC	European Economic Community (Common Market)
EU	European Union
FAIR	Federal Agricultural Improvement and Reform Act, 1996
FAO	Food and Agriculture Organisation (of the United Nations)
FNSEA	Fédération nationale des syndicats d'exploitants agricoles (National Federation of Farmers' Unions: FRSEA, FDSEA refer to regional or departmental groupings of the FNSEA)
FNSP	Fédération nationale des syndicates paysans (National Federation of Farmers Unions)
GATT	General Agreement on Tariffs and Trade
GMOs	Genetically modified organisms
IFAD	International Fund for Agricultural Development
LDCs	Less developed countries
MAI	Multilateral Agreement on Investment
NAFTA	North American Free Trade Agreement
PSE	Producer support estimate
ROPPA	Réseau des organisations paysannes et des producteurs de l'Afrique de l'ouest (West African Network of Small Farmer and Producer Organisations)
SAFER	Les Sociétés d'amenagement foncier et d'établissement rural (Associations for Land Management and Rural Settlement)
SCPs	Substitute cereal products
SCTL	Société civile des terres de Larzac (Larzac Land Association)
UPOV	L'Union internationale pour la protection des obtentions végétales (International Union for the Protection of New Varieties of Plants)
USDA	United States Department of Agriculture
WTO	World Trade Organisation

Translator's note

It has not proved easy to translate a work that deals with agri-culture from a French perspective into English. The history of French agriculture is radically different from that in Britain or the USA and many key terms are inherently problematic.

Of no term is this truer that *paysan*. Peasant, with all its pejorative associations in English, simply won't do. And farmer, while sometimes appropriate, often obscures nuances that matter by covering everyone from farm labourer to large-scale industrial entrepreneur at the producer end of the agri-food business chain. For the French, *paysan* carries many positive connotations, includ-ing a notion of having an organic connection to the land. It is true that from the 1950s onwards the dominant forces in French agriculture tried to reject the idea of *paysan* as passé. They opposed the terms *exploitant* or *agriculteur* to it, with the underlying assumption that the only proper farmers were 'modernisers' who treated their land as just another instrument of production (*outil de travail*), in contrast to *paysans*, who were merely backward-looking subsistence farmers for whom land was rather a 'family inheritance'.

The radical currents which came together into the Confédération Paysanne in the late 1980s consciously attempted to recuperate the word *paysan*, ridding it of its reactionary associations but keeping the senses of deep attachment to the land and stewardship as central to its meaning. Regenerated through their struggles, the word is once more in vogue even among those who previously

[x]

rejected it. I have rendered it variously as 'farmer', 'small farmer' or 'small, family farmer' according to the context. *Exploitant*, similarly, is translated variously as anything from 'farmer' to 'industrial manager'.

The Confédération Paysanne has also elaborated the concept of an *'agriculture paysanne'*, distinguished in every way from the productivist drive which characterises 'modern' industrial agriculture. The term is defined at some length in the Charter in Appendix 1. It is used to capture the notion of farming that is at once on a human scale and respectful of wider social and environmental considerations. I have translated it – very inadequately – as 'small farming' or occasionally as 'sustainable small farming' where the durability of this way of farming is emphasised.

The terms 'small farming' or 'family farming' are used today by the various trade unions that organise among those who practice this kind of agriculture. We find, for instance, the Small and Family Farms Alliance and the Family Farmers' Association in the UK, and the National Family Farm Coalition in the USA. I have nevertheless balked at using 'family farming' because of the hidden aspects of oppression within the family on such farms historically (though it is fair to say that its connotations in these circles today are pretty egalitarian).

The French also refer a lot to *'hors sol'* farming. This covers all kinds of traditional farming activities that now take place 'off soil', whether in battery farms and concrete buildings for animal rearing or in greenhouses (not quite off soil) for intensive vegetable production. The emphasis is on the fact that many of the items used in the production process do not come from the farm itself, that the location of such enterprises depends largely on economic factors such as proximity to motorways, ports, or urban centres of consumption rather than on the land itself. Whatever the nuances, the references in this book are always to processes that are intensive, industrial and chemicalised. 'Off soil' is bland, and the reality is captured by the term 'factory farming' which I use whenever the term occurs.

This book started out as a short booklet of around 20,000 words. It is more than twice as long now. The Confédération Paysanne were keen for it to appear in English, but acknowledged immediately that it needed adaptation. I was given a free hand to do so. I would like to acknowledge the generous help given in particular by Jean Damien Terreaux in the Confédération head office and by agricultural economist Jacques Berthelot who provided additional materials to expand and elaborate the argument in what have now become the first two chapters. Benoît Ducasse facilitated my original introduction to the Confédération and Jean-Marc Desfilhes, also of the Confédération, read and commented on parts of the translation. Finally, Gérard Choplin of Coordination Paysanne Européenne kindly advised on some of the technical terms. In addition, I have researched and added a fair amount of material myself, some to clarify the existing text and some of it entirely new, for example on the situation in the USA or Mexico, to elaborate the argument and/or to make it more relevant to an English-speaking readership.

I hope the final product is fully in line with the views of the Confédération and that, coming from a culture in which notions of the desirability of free trade and cheap food are imbibed from an early age, I have not distorted in any way the uncompromising opposition to both of these which is so richly justified in the analysis the Confédération has developed.

Finally, I would like to thank my editors at Pluto Press, Anne Beech and Dave Castle, for their support and Chris Carr of Curran Publishing Services for his prompt, courteous and supportive copy-editing.

Richard Kuper
London, June 2003

Foreword

'Free trade is the protectionism of the powerful.' In this elegant formulation Vandana Shiva, Indian fighter for peasant farmer rights, sums up her thinking in the face of those who ask her about the free-market economic policies favoured by the World Trade Organisation and the rich countries in general.

So too the Confédération Paysanne affirms that the free-market philosophy is anything but a project for the liberation of the men and women who live on this planet. Pushed to extremes, free-market society is the privatisation and transformation into commodities of everything that makes up the daily life of humankind, including all that is essential to life itself: water, the earth, seeds, the genetic heritage of humanity. This destructive system, based on the law that might is right, offers no future to billions of human beings, notably the peasants of the south for whom daily life is destitution and the hoe (or at best, animal-drawn implements).

Nor does this system offer any future to the small farmers of the North. Already they represent no more than 1 per cent of the population in Britain and the United States. The industrialisation of our societies, the deregulation and globalisation of trade and commerce, all coupled to the productivist development of agriculture, have signalled their virtual disappearance.

And yet. There are voices crying out, in every country of the world, becoming ever more numerous, that another world is possible: a world of solidarity, where wealth is fairly distributed, where the natural capital of the planet is not pillaged, a world in which commercial transactions are merely a tool to achieve these objectives and not an end in themselves.

We too subscribe to such a project. But we also believe that such a world is not possible without farmers. And more than that, it will be brought into being through the world's farmers, who represent a quarter of the population of our planet. On what basis do we, inhabitants of very rich and industrialised countries, hope to rebuild something other than the consumer society in which we live if that part of humanity that we represent has definitively broken its 'links with the land', delegating to a few agri-managers and a few agribusiness transnationals the entirety of our agricultural and food production?

That is why we affirm that the catastrophes that productivist and industrial agriculture have been responsible for over the last 40 years, in Europe and elsewhere, must not lead citizens to reject all forms of agricultural policy, as is often the case. The European Union, as it happens, is far from having tried everything. The project advocated by the Confédération Paysanne for many years, and advocated today by a number of substantial organisations throughout the world, proves that another agriculture is possible. It is also desirable and urgent.

And because we have the temerity to believe that what is true in the Latin countries is also true in the Anglo-Saxon ones and in the countries of the North, despite their different realities and histories, it is with great pleasure that we welcome the translation and adaption of this short book, originally published for a French-speaking audience, for an English-speaking readership. We trust that the debate launched here will feed our respective thinking about these concerns.

José Bové,
12 June 2003

Introduction

No one doubts there is a serious food problem in the world today. We see it in the 'mad cow' crisis and the consequent Creuzfeldt-Jacob disease in humans; we see it in pesticide pollution of our drinking water, life-threatening algae bloom in rivers enriched with fertiliser run-off, salmonella in chicken, or the drive towards genetically modified crops and foodstuffs. We see it also in the growth of junk food, obesity and associated illnesses in the industrialised world – and in the threat of famine in literally dozens of developing (or not developing) countries.

Yet regulation, essential to bringing this series of inter-related crises under control, has an increasingly bad name, at least in the mouths of politicians dedicated to 'freeing-up' markets, and in media representations of food and farming. Why? What has gone wrong? And what should be done about it?

This book emerges from the practice of the Confédération Paysanne, Europe's most important radical farmers' trade union, a union that won the support of 28 per cent of French farmers in elections in 2002. It locates the root of the problem in the logic of what it calls productivism in agriculture. This is the drive to increase output without limit and the consequent search for ever more 'efficient' methods of production. Agriculture has become a branch of industry, with escalating pressures to find new markets for its burgeoning output. This transformation of farming is recent. It has occurred essentially since the 1950s, in large parts of Europe, North and South America, Australia and elsewhere under a variety of different agricultural regimes.

All countries have traditionally subsidised their agricultural systems, a primordial function of government being to keep their populations from starvation. In the newly formed Common Market, the form of protection chosen was guaranteed prices without any limitation on output. This may have been an understandable choice, given strong memories of post-war famine in Europe. But, as the analysis in this book shows, it was a disastrous one. Output exploded and Europe was soon awash with milk and wine lakes surrounded by beef and butter mountains. Many aspects of the Common Agricultural Policy contributed to making it an ongoing disaster for European – and indeed world – agriculture.

The distribution of subsidies and supports among farmers was iniquitous; the larger the farm the more it benefited from the subsidies. The Common Agricultural Policy became a way of funding 'industrialised' farmers at the expense of the rest, an instrument for forcing small farmers off the land in the interests of 'efficient' farming. 'Successful' farmers were increasingly integrated into the ever more powerful national and then transnational agribusiness corporations which have come to dominate the sector. Such farmers might, for example, get their seed from the same company that supplies their fertiliser, herbicide and pesticide needs and purchases their output (at a price set by the company). At the same time, the European Community did a deal with the USA, which accepted the Common Market arrangements in exchange for duty-free access for its soya and other animal feedstuffs. Without such cheap feed in Europe, the factory farm transformation of meat and poultry production could never have occurred as it did.

With the arrival of food surpluses, rather than shortage, Europe's export drive was launched. But for the traded goods to be competitive, producers have to be paid to export and this the CAP did lavishly with its system of restitutions. The result was the dumping on world markets of food from Europe (and elsewhere) at prices far below the real production costs in the countries concerned. Theoretically outlawed by the GATT, dumping was and remains a central feature of the exports of virtually all developed countries.

The World Trade Organisation and its Agreement on Agriculture are founded on the dogma that free trade works to create wealth for everyone. This has no truth whatsoever in the realm of agriculture. In a complex set of arrangements, known as red, green, amber and blue boxes, subsidies in agriculture have been classified and graded in terms of their supposed trade-distorting effects and we are moving towards a system in which only so-called non-distorting supports are allowed. As this book shows, this is a con and its effects are disastrous. Developing countries are being forced to open their markets to imports in basic commodities in which they are self-sufficient, leading to massive disruption to their small farmers and thus to their ability to feed themselves. Food dumping continues apace and food security is being sacrificed on the altar of free trade. In this the USA is as guilty as the EU, although its massive subsidies to agriculture largely pass the test of being supposedly non-trade-distorting.

The chief beneficiary of this largesse is not, as might appear, the general farming community; this is as true in the USA as it is in Europe. Who then benefits? National and transnational agribusiness, the ICIs, Monsantos, Cargills, Nestlés and Carrefours of this world. As this analysis shows clearly, the price is paid not just by the mass of subsistence and small peasant farmers of the developing world but by the small farmers of the industrialised world as well. The enormous subsidies being poured into agriculture pass through the hands of the farmers and end up in the pockets of agribusiness. Small farmers are rapidly being forced out of farming, as a matter of conscious policy. The price of food bears no relation to its real costs of production, social and environmental costs of intensive agriculture are not factored in at all, and the taxpayer ends up footing the bill.

The favoured solution of governments like those of Britain – unregulated trade – would be a disaster for rural communities, for what is left of farming as a way of life, for the quality and safety of food, and for the environment, as the transnationals consolidate their hold worldwide and seek production at the lowest possible price.

What is the alternative? Here the experience of the Confédération Paysanne comes into its own. Emerging out of small farmers' struggles in France in the 1970s and 1980s, the Confédération Paysanne has been instrumental in developing alternative policies for agriculture and in working with others at the European level (through the Coordination Paysanne Européenne) and the world level (through Via Campesina). It has initiated a whole variety of militant actions: protesting against the GATT/WTO long before most people realised how significant it was; opposing genetically modified seed production through actions that included a series of high profile digging up of secretive crop trials. Not to forget the inspired 'dismantling' of McDonald's in Millau in 1999 which first drew the world's attention to the Confédération Paysanne and to its high profile, mediagenic spokesperson José Bové.

Militantly involved in struggles against the domination of industrialised agriculture, the Conf (as it affectionately known) has struggled hard and consistently to look after the interests of small farmers everywhere. But not, as the dominant union in France has done, by putting self-interest (in its case the self-interest of the large grain, beef and sugar barons) above the interests of society as a whole. The Confédération Paysanne has developed a set of alternative policies for a small farmers' agriculture, linking together the interests of small farmers and rural communities in being able to prosper without destroying the environment, with those of the general population in having quality food to consume, and with those of the mass of small farmers in developing countries in not having their possibility of survival destroyed by dumped food.

For that to be possible an alternative is needed to both the existing Common Agricultural Policy and to the proposed alternative of free trade (with some environmental protection add-ons – what the Conf calls 'green liberalism'). The Agreement on Agriculture has to be recognised for the disaster it is, especially from a developing countries' perspective. The Confédération Paysanne spells out the principles involved in a move towards an alternative, a solidaristic citizens' and farmers' CAP. It calls for the abandoning of the supposed export vocation of agriculture in the European Union, concentrating rather on food for internal consumption and only high-value added quality products for export; an intelligent protectionism; planning for food sovereignty on a regional level; supply management of agricultural produce, whose aim is to produce in relation to internal demand and to keep the maximum number of farmers in production rather than the minimum by redistributing the quantities agreed as desirable among farmers and regions of Europe. For this to be possible a policy of adequate prices is needed. Farmers must be able to earn enough to sustain their activities (including their 'multifunctional' environmental ones) without forcing them to degrade their lives, food quality and the countryside as is the current norm. A de-intensified agriculture is called for, one that produces less but better, one that keeps the countryside peopled and respects nature, one that integrates agricultural policy into rural policy in order to revitalise the countryside. What is needed is to move away from the policies of enlargement, concentration and industrialisation, and to put small farms back into the heart of agriculture.

Such a policy would favour farmers, food sovereignty and food security in developing countries as well. Rather than encouraging the destructive switch towards export agriculture in developing countries which is occurring at breakneck pace at the expense of the mass of small farmers there, these policies would allow such countries to look after their own food needs and to have full freedom to protect their agricultures from cheap food being dumped on to them.

In shifting to such an alternative agriculture, transitional arrangements would be essential. Subsidies should be capped according to farm size and distributed in favour of those who need them, rather than in favour of those who already have plenty (which is precisely what occurs at present where the richest 20 per cent of farmers received 80 per cent of CAP monies). At the same time, social and environmental criteria are essential in determining the distribution of subsidies, which must serve goals that society as a whole approves of and wishes to encourage.

Such policies, so this book contends, can provide a viable, sustainable alternative to the ravages of industrial agriculture. They could favour the interests of producer and consumer, the interests of the mass of small farmers in the developed and the developing world at one and the same time. A win–win arrangement could replace the current lose-lose one; or one in which the citizens of the world win by curbing the powers of the transnationals.

Richard Kuper

1 The industrialisation of farming

The main challenge facing Europe after the Second World War was to become self-sufficient in food. It had a long way to go. More food had to be produced with less labour as a result of a drift away from the land that had accelerated rapidly after the First World War. At the same time there was also a need to recruit the labour necessary for industrial development as 'modernisation' programmes succeeded one another.

At the international level, the Treaty of Rome established the foundations of the European Economic Community in 1957. At the national level in France, the various agricultural guidance laws (lois d'orientation agricole, LOAs) of 1960 and 1962 gave a clarion call for the accelerated 'modernisation' of agriculture. Annuities for those withdrawing from farming (a sort of retirement gift to those over 65) freed up a good number of farms; favourable loans subsidised by the government stimulated the purchase of equipment and the construction of larger buildings; 'Associations for Land Management and Rural Settlement' (les Sociétés d'amenagement foncier et d'établissement rural, or SAFER) were established to acquire land put up for sale and use it to aid consolidation of holdings or set up young farmers in agriculture. A logic of intensification – the need to produce more on the same amount of land – took hold with its corollaries of mechanisation and specialisation. Subsidising the consolidation of land holdings was to launch a vicious circle, a permanent restructuring of agriculture forcing an incessant exodus of farmers, a haemorrhaging which was to bleed a goodly number of French and European regions.

The situation in Britain was not much different. The 1947 Agricultural Act guaranteed markets and prices in exchange for increased efficiency, encouraged further in the 1957 Act. The effect was that there was a similar fall in the number of people on the land as 'modernisation' proceeded apace.[1]

At the end of the 1940s, there were still 3 million farmers in France. All were involved in the call to produce more. No bounds were set; supposedly there was to be an unlimited increase in output. This was the heyday of mechanisation; the train of 'progress' was on the move. Farmers became industrial producers, and they weren't going to fail to produce.

1962: the birth of productivism

The birth of the Common Agricultural Policy (CAP) was not without its difficulties. The six European countries that had signed the Treaty of Rome – France, Germany, Italy, the Netherlands, Belgium and Luxemburg – had very different agricultures in terms of size of farms, degrees of mechanisation, yields, costs of production and so on. After many years of negotiation the CAP, which had been agreed merely in relation to the broadest of goals in the Treaty of Rome in 1957, finally saw the light of day under the aegis of Sicco Mansholt, former Minister of Agriculture in the Netherlands. It was based on three founding principles:

- A single market: agricultural products would be able to circulate freely within the Common Market, once the elimination of customs controls, taxes and other national subsidies had been agreed. Regulations of all sorts were to be harmonised and the price of products to be the same everywhere within the market.

- Community preference: agricultural price levels within the EEC were to be guaranteed at levels generally above those of the world market. Any product imported into the EEC would be subject to a variable levy, an import tax that corresponded to the difference between its price on entry and the Community price. To sell outside the EEC and to compensate for the difference between (lower) world and European price levels, an export subsidy was to be paid out, known as a refund or restitution. Thanks to this system, the supply of food for member countries of the Community was to be provided, first and foremost, from within the internal market. This protection was rapidly to become a source of contention with the large agricultural exporting countries such as Australia, Canada and of course the United States.

- Financial solidarity: the European Agricultural Guidance and Guarantee Fund (EAGGF) was created. All states contributed to it in relation to their wealth and collectively took control of its expenditure, which ranged over everything from improving farm structures through mechanisms for dealing with crises, to the purchase, storage and disposal of surpluses through exporting.

Alongside these lofty principles for regulating the Common Market, the first common market organisations emerged, notably for cereals and beef. They were based on a price policy, hinged on a target price fixed annually (a maximum price) and an intervention price (a minimum price). The public authority had the power to intervene in order to stabilise prices by buying and storing output when the internal price fell below the intervention price, in order to bring about a rise in price levels.[2] Price support was thus linked to state intervention. It was not a new idea: France, for instance, had tried such a system of controlling markets with the creation of the Interprofessional National Wheat Board (the ONIB) in 1936, as had Britain with its Milk Marketing Board.

The consequences of this policy materialised quickly enough: productivity rose and production exploded. Once the productivist model was in place the goal of self-sufficiency was soon achieved, and then rapidly passed. (The term productivism is used throughout to describe the new system of commercialised agriculture in which maximising outputs takes precedence over all other considerations, whether of a social, health or environmental nature.) Launched in great haste, the productivist policy left an increasing number of farmers by the wayside. The destruction of jobs and an increasing concentration of production were directly linked to an absence of political will to control production and competition among European farmers, who were soon caught up in the spiral of trade globalisation.

Once the process of basic mechanisation had been successfully accomplished, intensive agriculture asserted itself. It relied on a massive use of inputs – fertilisers, feed-stuffs, phytosanitary products (products concerned with the health of plants, such as pesticides and fungicides) and so on – and turned out more and more produce for transformation by the burgeoning agribusiness industries.

Beyond Europe the consequences for so-called developing countries were particularly severe. Subsidised exports came to compete unfairly with local producers, undermining local products. From now on farmers worldwide were in competition with each other. A drastic fall in the number of farmers on the European continent and abroad became unavoidable, while within the EEC the mechanism of unlimited price support opened the way to spiralling over-production.

Exporting and free trade

The choice of this interventionist policy arose in fact from a political compromise reached in 1961 between the EEC and the United States in the Dillon Round of the General Agreement on Tariffs and Trade (the GATT Agreement) in 1961–62.

The very existence of the EEC went against the grain of the postwar free-market order, but customs unions were exempted from the normal application of GATT rules (which otherwise insisted that any trading concession granted to one member had to be granted to all others). At the same time, for political reasons, the USA was in favour of broader European unity. So, while it would have preferred unrestricted access to foreign markets, the USA was prepared to accept the closure of the European Economic Community's agricultural markets, especially after a sweetener was conceded. The EEC's right to protect food products traditionally produced on a large scale (such as cereals, milk, beef, or sugar) by variable levies on imports and by export refunds was accepted. But, in return, Europe effectively ceded to the USA the right to produce soya for animal feed. This was thought to be marginal at the time. This approach was confirmed a few years later in the Kennedy Round (1962–67) when Europe allowed the duty-free importation of 'substitute cereal products' (SCPs).[3]

This deal was to have fateful consequences. The double scale of prices thus introduced encouraged European farmers to produce what was protected and rewarding (principally cereals) and to buy in from abroad what had become cheap for animal feed (soya and SCPs). And among the main productions protected by the new system, there was a hierarchy of guaranteed prices that profited producers of cereals more than producers of meats (agreed under German pressure since their cereal prices were the highest in Europe and they did not wish their farmers to suffer a drop in income). This had the further consequence of accelerating the importation of SCPs, to the detriment of European cereals which were largely squeezed out of the animal feedstuffs market at home.

As a result, meat production rapidly became industrialised and factory-farm enterprises for intensive livestock and poultry production sprang up near ports (particularly in Brittany, Catalonia, the Netherlands and Belgium). Firms producing feedstuffs developed the battery production of chickens and veal using hormones. And, at the same time, Europe came to sacrifice its independence in vegetable protein production.

The phenomenon of runaway over-production, provoked by productivist politics at the Community level, pushed states to turn to the world market in search of outlets for their surpluses. Budgetary costs continued to soar because of the commitment to taking the ever-increasing surpluses into storage. Internal outlets were soon saturated and the targeting of external markets became inevitable. As already noted, the principle of exporting European agricultural surpluses was written into the CAP from its foundations in 1962. The postwar period was one in which liberal free-market principles blossomed. After some haggling this had been expressed in the framework of the GATT, established in 1948, four years after the creation of the World Bank and the IMF, following the Bretton Woods Accords. The philosophy of the GATT – since 1995 the World Trade Organisation (WTO) – is simple: free trade encourages economic growth and contributes to prosperity for all. Even if trade in agricultural produce was only very partially within its remit, it was none the less significantly affected. The GATT/WTO's objective has always been clear: to lower tariff barriers on both primary and manufactured products, a principle applied increasingly during the course of eight successive rounds of negotiations.

Discussions in the WTO rest on the notion of treating 'similar products' in the same way, looking only at the product as such, without reference to methods of production. As a result it becomes impossible to subordinate trade to social or ecological norms. Here looms the 'brave new world' of the neoliberal model.

Box 1.1: WTO 'similar product' rules

The WTO is particularly concerned with eliminating non-tariff barriers to trade: that is, regulatory measures of one kind or another which restrict or limit trade. Its two agreements – one on technical barriers to trade, the other on sanitary and phytosanitary measures – both say they are about harmonising standards and rules for the protection of the environment, public health and consumers. But in practice this means imposing ceilings, not floors, on what national governments can do. The bottom line is that no account may be taken of the 'processes and methods of production' when considering imports from other WTO member countries.

Its effects are increasingly felt. Already two of the EU's key animal welfare achievements – the prohibition on the import of furs from countries using the leghold trap and the ban on the marketing of cosmetics tested on animals – have been substantially modified to avoid a challenge under WTO rules. In addition, Compassion in World Farming points out that WTO rules are making it increasingly difficult for the EU (or any other WTO member) to introduce good new animal welfare measures. It is true that the EU can prohibit a cruel rearing system within its own territory. However, the fact that under WTO rules it cannot prohibit the import of meat or eggs derived from animals reared in that system in third countries acts as a powerful disincentive to the EU prohibiting that system within its own territory.[4]

The problem is simply that under WTO rules how something is produced is not generally regarded as a relevant consideration. Yet, from an animal welfare point of view, say, this is *the* issue. For the WTO, an egg is just an egg. Even if a country wants to prohibit battery-rearing at home, it is not allowed to extend this ban to imported eggs. As Compassion in World Farming puts it:

> This leads to the absurdity that, starting off from a rule that imported products cannot be discriminated against, we arrive at the position where imported products must be treated more favourably than domestic ones. For example, a WTO member can prohibit the marketing of domestically produced stall and tether-pigmeat, but cannot extend that ban to imported pigmeat.[5]

The new WTO disputes procedure is incredibly harsh. Its panels consist of 'experts' whose names are not disclosed and who meet behind closed doors. A decision can only be set aside by the unanimous agreement of all WTO members – including the country that brought the case!

The emerging jurisprudence of the GATT/WTO is, not surprisingly, unencouraging. Actions like the banning of imports of tuna caught in drift nets rather than with rod and line, the EU favouring former colonies when it comes to the importing of bananas, or prohibiting the import of hormone-fed beef, have all fallen foul of the WTO. Controls over trade in toxic waste, or on trade in endangered species (supposedly regulated by CITES) are likely to be increasingly called into question.

Even US legislation has fallen foul of the new system, as US corporate interests use it to batter down previously established systems of national protection. Thus the Federal Meat Inspection Act, amended in 1978 to ensure that meat and meat products imported into the USA are from livestock slaughtered in accordance with methods permitted under the

Federal Humane Slaughter Act, is invalidated under the WTO view that meat is simply meat; the notion of 'similar products' does not take the process of slaughter into account.

Similarly, the President's power (under the Pelly amendment) to embargo wildlife and wildlife products from nations that have diminished the effectiveness of international conservation agreements such as CITES would almost certainly be challenged if there were an attempt to use it against a WTO member state.

Or again, look at the US plan to phase out all use of asbestos. It fell foul of the US–Canada Free Trade Agreement, when challenged by Canada, a major asbestos producer. It was not that the health risks of asbestos were not recognised but it was ruled that banning it was not 'the least trade-restrictive solution'!

From stockpiling to commercial war

The first crises of over-production appeared at the end of the 1960s: rivers of milk, mountains of butter, fridges stuffed full of meat. Postwar governments had defended agricultural prices above those of the world market, but they also wanted prices low enough to satisfy their electorates.

In reality, the policy of agricultural price support from 1962 to 1992 was more restrictive than generally presented. Except for a short period of five years between 1972 and 1977, the purchasing power of farmers, compared to that of other social groups, fell steadily.

The only response ever on the agenda within the Common Market was to pursue the logic of intensification: that is, to reduce the number of producers, and increase the average size of farm units. From 1955 to 1970 the so-called 'agricultural area in use' in France rose by 45 per cent per farm (from 14.1 to 20.4 hectares).[6] A commission, presided over by the highly-respected figure of Georges Vedel, a Professor of constitutional law in Paris, prepared a report on the 'Long-term perspectives for French agriculture, 1968–85' as a contribution to the preparation of the Sixth Plan. For the first time the idea was floated of 'setting aside' land (i.e. leaving it fallow) in order to reduce over-production, a proposal envis-aged for a third of the area then used for farming, or some 11 million hectares. To this enchanting proposition was added a reduction of a similar order in the number of people active in farming: the Vedel Report suggested 600–700,000 survivors of the 2 million then active in French farming.

At the European level, the Mansholt Plan of 1968 followed the same logic: the rate at which the farming popu-lation was falling was not nearly fast enough, so farmers were to be encouraged to withdraw from farming, small farms to be consolidated, the total amount of land farmed reduced considerably and productivity on what remained increased. To do this, governments, which controlled the finance tap, had an unanswerable weapon: financial subventions. Whether it was a matter of loans or subsidies, the thumbs-up signal was only given to farmers judged 'competent' and 'dynamic' in terms of criteria like their abil-ity to draw up a development plan, to follow training courses and to keep accounts.

The main victims of what Madeleine Lefrançois called at the time the 'hunt for small farmers' were traditional artisan farmers, practising polyculture and animal husbandry, and subsistence producers, a large part of whose output was consumed on the spot.[7] They were roundly condemned in the forecasts made by economists of the period in relation to how they saw the evolution of farm structures during the period 1963–85. Their number was slashed at the stroke of the experts' pen from 1 million to 100,000: simply to be reduced to a tenth in a period of 20 years. With competi-tiveness without limit as the goal, these smallholders were being given a choice of slow suffocation or sudden death. At

the same time, the two other categories used in this classifi-
cation, neo-artisanal producers and capitalist farmers – that
is, those deemed 'dynamic' or industrialised – saw their
potential numbers growing over the same period.

While the experts laboured, the farmers produced.
Europe tottered under its stocks of 700,000 tonnes of butter
and a million tonnes of milk powder. These repeated crises
of over-production eventually led to the first quotas – on
milk – in 1984.

In 1983 about 30 per cent of the agricultural guarantee
fund had gone towards milk products (largely the subsidising of exports and the storing of surplus butter and
skimmed milk powder, themselves eventually to be
dumped on the world market). To reduce this drain a reduction of around 9 per cent was proposed in milk production,
with drastic penalties for farmers who overproduced. These
restrictions were to allow the market to be regulated by
adjusting supply to demand and by guaranteeing a price
acceptable to the producer.

The distribution of these quotas among producers and
countries was done with reference to past history, which had
the effect of ratifying the injustices done to small and medium
producers. They were not guilty of over-production, while
the champions of quantitative performance benefited further
from their quasi-monopoly rent position. It was an attempt to
control the amount produced, and caused outrage among
those who regarded market 'freedom' as sacrosanct.

Despite the possibilities held out by the introduction of
quotas, European agricultural policy did not rid itself of its
productivist blinkers. Because producers could no longer
produce as much as they wanted, the only way to maximise
production now was by eliminating others: pushing a
certain number over the edge was enough to restore the
opportunities for those remaining. So, the milk quotas did
nothing to limit the concentration of production: thanks to

financial incentives (in the form of subsidies for getting out of dairy farming), the number of milk producers in France fell from 440,000 in 1983 to 125,000 by 2000. In the EU-9, the number of dairy-cow holdings declined even further after 1984: from 4.1 per cent per year between 1975 and 1984 to 4.6 per cent per year between 1985 and 1997. (EU statistics relate to the number countries in the EU at the time, indicated by the description EU-6, EU-9, EU-10, EU-12, EU-15 etc.) The system of increased output per worker in farming continued and the size of dairy farms in France tripled between 1984 and 2002.

Entire areas were abandoned. Production became increasingly concentrated in the most developed regions, while the number of farmers in difficulty grew and environmental problems, linked principally to damage caused by consolidation of holdings, emerged. Nitrate run-off from concentrated production units is a particular example.

An intensified competition emerged – between producers, between regions, between countries – based on a commercial war that was reflected in increasingly fierce international negotiations.

The logic of free trade

During the course of the GATT round launched in 1986 at Punta del Este (hence the name, the Uruguay Round), four new strategic sectors, previously left in the remit of 'national sovereignty', were introduced into the negotiations: services, intellectual property rights, trade-related investment and agriculture. This last was to lead to a prolonged trial of strength between the USA and the European Union. Apart from these superpowers, the only countries to intervene in the debate were the 14 countries of the so-called Cairns Group whose members (notably Australia, New Zealand, Canada, Argentina and Brazil) defined themselves as 'fair' exporters, that is to say ones who did not subsidise their exports. Developing counties were unable to get their specific concerns taken into account at all. (In particular, despite the important work of the committee on tropical products during the Uruguay Round, their problems were not even mentioned in the final agreement.)

The negotiatiors of the Uruguay Round took it upon themselves to generalise the logic of free trade to agriculture. But the logic of free trade rests on four major mystifications that need to be examined more closely.

First, according to neoliberal dogma, agricultural markets are self-regulating. This claim is not supported by the facts. For example, over the last decade or so the large industrialised countries have substantially increased their openness to world markets, yet markets have not stabilised as a result. On the contrary, their instability has been particularly marked. Contrary to the neoliberal credo, agricultural markets have a spontaneous and chaotic character. Public intervention is thus necessary to assure their regulation, to adjust the evolution of prices and to guarantee the remuneration of producers: the only way to maintain agricultural activity.

While demand may be stable in the short run, agricultural production fluctuates according to climatic vagaries. Agricultural prices and incomes fluctuate even more, as do consumer prices. That is why all countries since the time of the Pharaohs have had agricultural policies to regulate agricultural supply, both at the level of imports and by having some storage policy to minimise price fluctuations. The world market, given its domination by agri-food oligopolies (see below), is unable to provide the regulation needed. Rules of international coordination other than the free trade fostered by the WTO are required. Regulatory stocks of tropical products (coffee, cocoa, rubber) existed formerly under international agreements. Their suppression since the end of the 1980s has caused their world prices to collapse to historic lows, ruining tens of millions of farmers in developing countries and preventing any possibility of economic development. And the dismantling of supply management measures in the USA since 1996 (see Box 5.1) is the main reason for the slump in prices of grains (cereals and oilseeds) and even cotton. This is even more important than the high US and EU agricultural subsidies.

Second, there is the claim that competition creates wealth for all. Perhaps it is not out of place to ask what sense there is to competition that involves both the disappearance of competitors and the destruction of the capacity to produce? Sheep farming in France testifies to this development: almost 12,500 sheep farmers of the 66,340 in 1993 left the land within the next five years. The disproportionate scale of this loss is underlined by the fact that the EU – and France in particular – has a growing trade deficit in sheepmeat. What makes the situation even worse is the vital role of sheep farming to the economy and environment of remote and mountainous areas.

In agriculture, the gap between the productivity of labour in subsistence farming in poor countries (10 quintals of cereals per active worker per year) and mechanised market production in the rich countries (10,000 quintals per active worker per year) is of the order of 1 to 1,000. It would be laughable to claim their encounter in the same market as fair and honest were the consequences not so drastic for those who end up flooding into the shanty towns of the mega-cities of the entire planet. We are talking here of the idea of fair and equal exchange between the overwhelming majority of peasant farmers (1.3 billion agricultural workers worldwide) practising manual or animal-assisted production and a 28-million mechanised minority armed for exporting – and among whom the most productive benefit from subsidies of all kinds.

The idea that French cereal production is particularly productive is also based on myth: in the period 1992–99 the 13,000 largest of the 75,000 cereal farms in France received on average, over €32,900 a year in direct aid per active worker – around a hundred times as much as Somalian peasant farmers receive for their entire harvest.

In reality, the great beneficiaries of this mystification are the agri-food industries and the transnationals, which can always acquire their basic inputs in large quantity at very low prices.

Third is the famous 'world price', said to be the criterion around which production should be oriented. Jacques Berthelot has provided a full discussion of the limitations of any such reliance.[8] Such prices are both extremely unstable and substantially 'dumped'; in other words, they are the prices of goods sold at well below their full production costs. It is therefore impossible to rely on these prices as credible signals to producers. In addition, this price covers only a very small part of world production and consumption. World exports of wheat in the period 1985–98 were 19.9 per cent of world production, rice 4.5 per cent, meat as a whole 8.9 per cent and dairy products 10.5 per cent; and these figures include trade between EU member states as part of world trade.[9]

Comparable figures for the period 1995–98, but excluding trade between EU member states, show world exports of wheat at 14.7 per cent of world production, rice at 5.6 per cent, meat as a whole at 8.2 per cent and dairy products at 6.4 per cent of world production. Why, it should be asked, should trade that is such a tiny proportion of world production and sales of these foodstuffs determine their prices everywhere?

Furthermore, in what sense are these world market prices real prices? In effect, international exchanges take place at prices that are not determined by the totality of these exchanges, but at the price of the most 'competitive' exporting country, a price that is almost always a 'dumping' price that is only possible thanks to significant subsidies received by agricultural exporters. From this it follows that a world price structurally set below the costs of production of the richest regions cannot in any event be the reference point around which agricultural policy should revolve.

On top of all this, it must be remembered that world food prices make no provision for the effects of either social or ecological dumping. For example, knowing that the US domestic oil price is a quarter that of France or Germany, and remembering that the USA accounts for 25 per cent of the world's greenhouse effects (with only 4 per cent of the world's population), it is obvious that most of its agri-food products – not to speak of others – would not be competitive if it were to increase its domestic oil price significantly so as to internalise part of these greenhouse effects.

Remember, too, that much world trade in foodstuffs is controlled by transnationals in a sector in which concentration of ownership is increasing rapidly.[10] This allows firms the opportunity of both manipulating prices to force competitors out of business, and of monopolising the marketing of the product, which means that the return to small farmers who sell their produce to these sole buyers can be forced lower and lower.

Box 1.2: The 'world prices' of dairy products[11]

These prices are particularly meaningless. To consider New Zealand's dairy prices as the world reference price is absurd, not only because this country accounts for only 2.2 per cent of world milk production but also because it is a 'price taker', that is, its dairy prices are fixed a little below those of dairy products exported – with high refunds – by the EU, which remains the world's major exporter. Admittedly New Zealand has a true competitiveness since it really does not subsidise its producers, but they enjoy exceptionally favourable ecological conditions for milk production and have large economies of scale (271 dairy cows per farm on average and a quasi-monopoly with 96 per cent of the market controlled by a single cooperative), but, exporting 90 per cent of its production already, it probably does not have significant possibilities for expanding it.

To treat the gap between the domestic farm price and the world (here New Zealand) price as 'subsidies' from consumers to farmers (what mainstream theory calls the negative 'consumers' surplus', assuming that consumers are entitled to pay the world price) could just be conceivable for a single small country whose share of the world consumption is not significant. Applying this to *all* consumers, as the OECD does, is an enormous mistake. The more so since the use of the 'world' price is not limited to the share of traded products in OECD (or world) production (6.4 per cent for dairy products at the world level, most of it intra-OECD) but to the entire world's consumption. It is clear that the world price would be completely different from the New Zealand price if the entire world dairy output were traded – an absurd hypothesis, incidentally. Indeed Maurice Doyon et al. have shown that the true world reference prices of dairy products derived from a world economic model of free trade should be US domestic prices, which are in fact comparable with EU prices![12]

The OECD's Producer Support Estimate (PSE) indicator portrays the EU as 'subsidising' its dairy sector by €19.2 billion in 1999 and €16.1 billion in 2001 (the years taken by Doyon et al.), or €190 per tonne of milk in 1999. But this concept of PSE is biased in two ways. First. it treats as 'subsidies' not merely the actual EU expenditure on the dairy chain (€2.5 billion in 1999) but also the negative 'consumers' surplus'. So for 1999 the actual subsidies (€2.5 billion) represent only 13 per cent of the dairy PSE (€19.2 billion), the negative 'consumers' surplus' representing 87 per cent. Hence, of the PSE expressed as euros per tonne, the subsidies part is worth around €25 and the negative 'consumers' surplus' part €165 out of a total of €190. Second, if the world price is meaningless – because it is a dumped price below the production cost of almost every country – so too is the calculation of the 'consumers' subsidy' that is based on it. Using the US price of milk as the true reference price, Doyon shows that the EU's PSE per tonne of milk turns out to be not €190, but €28. On this basis, EU consumers are subsidised by EU farmers, who do not get the fair price they should if you consider that the world price should be a free-trade price! We do not. We cannot agree with a concept of PSE that assumes consumers everywhere are entitled to pay a 'world price', which is generally a highly dumped price, and moreover a highly volatile one. The more so since, when producer prices are lowered to the world price levels there is no automatic reduction in consumer prices at all. For example, when EU cereals prices were lowered to the world price level after 1993, consumer prices did *not* follow suit; the 'surplus' was simply appropriated by the agri-food industries! This explains the complaint of French milk producers who were still being paid the same price in 2002 as they had received in 1989.

Despite this, many reform groups have fallen for the mystifications of the PSE. Based on the OECD figure, Oxfam writes on the front page of its report *Milking the CAP* that 'European citizens are supporting the dairy industry to the tune of €16 billion a year. This is equivalent to more than $2 [around €2.25] per cow per day – half the world's people live on less than this amount.'[13] This figure was immediately used by the chair of the World Bank, appeared on the front page of *Le Monde* and was cited by trade policy analyst Duncan Green of CAFOD in response to the CAP deal of June 2003.[14]

The actual EU dairy subsidy amounts only to around one-seventh of this figure or €0.34 per cow (€2.5 billion divided by 20.4 million dairy cows and by 365 days). This is nevertheless still too high when we know that on average three-quarters of it is a direct or indirect subsidy to dairy exports.

It is not just direct export subsidies that have distorting effects on world prices. Decoupled supports (i.e. supports not linked directly to output) do so too, and there are yet other factors that amount to subsidies that have to be taken into account. Public expenditure for example, particularly on transport infrastructure, significantly influences the price at which commodities are marketed. It is in effect another subsidy which affects international competitiveness and the so-called world price.

Fourth and finally, there is the 'hard core' of the neoliberal mantra: free trade is claimed to be the engine of economic development. On the contrary, we see that exports are hardly the panacea for bringing about development. Exporting countries keep only a small part of the revenues generated by exports. Most profits are made in the process of adding value, not in producing the primary materials; and the revenues that accrue to the growers of this primary produce are further reduced when they have to import the technical means needed (equipment, fertilisers, phytosanitary products) to improve their productivity. In such circumstances local incomes decrease while the expenses associated with imports rise. In reality, lower tariffs generate a lower rise in imports than does an increase in income and in consumption. Under cover of openness, the dismantling of import controls exacerbates competition between producers and merely favours export crops at the expense of subsistence agriculture.

Neoliberal free market ideology assumes it is a good thing for subsistence and small surplus-producing (read 'inefficient') farmers to go to the wall. Most of their outputs are generally not commoditised (i.e. turned into commodities for sale on the market) and therefore do not show up in national GDP statistics. They are therefore assumed to be without value. There is no concept of the human cost to people who, once able to feed themselves and their families and contribute to the welfare of their local communities, can no longer do so.

The USA, in accordance with its pure and uncompromising neoliberal vision, has European export subsidies in its sights. It wants to impose the dictates of competition on agricultural markets and to undermine the very possibility of Europe regulating its internal market. On the essential issue, it is joined by the Cairns Group, which favours the idea of decoupling subsidies in agriculture: the policy of price support would be replaced by a policy of direct, decoupled aid, said not to have an effect on production. Of course it has an effect on production: farmers who can draw a substantial income from direct aid can afford to produce and sell crops they otherwise could not. But only rich countries can afford to subsidise their farmers directly in this way. Control of imports is in effect the only politics of solidarity, because it is available at zero cost to poor countries.

American negotiators also proposed an 'option zero' during the first phase of the Uruguay Round negotiations, consisting of the suppression of all forms of aid for exports and, more broadly, for agriculture in general by the end of the year 2000, a proposal rejected by the European negotiators who wished for a progressive reduction globally of agricultural supports. The tension remains strong between the two blocs, both of which are looking for ways of releasing their surpluses onto the world market. Negotiations were even suspended in 1990. We already know the losers: developing countries out-competed in their own markets by dumped surpluses.

The USA brandishes the threat of closing its frontiers, made possible by a new commercial law, the Trade Act, adopted in 1988 in order to pressurise the EU into adopting a policy of income (in place of price) support. It is a game of liars' poker because farmers in most developed countries benefit from protectionism, whether financed by consumers (via guaranteed prices) or by taxpayers (via subsidies given to farmers or to agribusiness). Whatever the outcome, the European logic remains unchanged: reduce costs of production and prices and thereby restructure agriculture, that is to say, persist in the logic of rural depopulation that is destroying the countryside, in order to maintain a high level of competitiveness. Over the ruins, European decision-makers and agri-managers continue unperturbed to intone their hymn to the world market and the export vocation of European, and particularly French, agriculture.

Box 1.3: On poultry for plucking

The Doux group is the foremost French and European producer of poultry and ranks third in the world, with a turnover of €1.6 billion in 2001 and a production of 1.1 million tons of poultry products in 2002. It knows all about exporting: with its exports reaching 140 countries, that is its obsession. In the 1930s chicken from Nantes was sold in Paris, then in Switzerland and Germany; now the major outlet is the Middle East. The Doux empire is based on integration. At one end of the chain is the poultry rearer, whom Doux supplies with young chicks and their feedstuffs before buying back the birds under conditions it controls. At the other end of the chain, it controls the refrigerator ships and the abattoirs. Why then such insistence on turning to the world market where prices are very low and where the ups and downs of the international conjuncture make exports yo-yo wildly (the collapse of Iraqi and Iranian markets at the end of the 1980s, for example, followed by the Russian and Asiatic crises of the 1990s)?

Rest assured, the emperor of the drumstick has not gone mad. It simply does not care about the wild competition its exports provoke on local production (the collapse of prices, and ruin of peasants who take a one-way ticket to the nearest shanty town). It does not lose any sleep over the social dumping practised by the new exporting countries to lower their costs of production. The logic is simple: it is sucking up European subsidies, baptised as restitutions, in other words public funds.

But doesn't the Agreement on Agriculture envisage a decline in these? Yes, and an alternative is already available for when this no longer works. It is called delocalisation – in the direction of wherever regulatory constraints of an environmental and social kind are lowest. Thus Doux has already bought Frangosul, the fourth largest poultry producer in Brazil, where costs of production are about two-thirds what they are in France: around €0.76 a kilo as against €1.14. Even if one third of the Breton poultry farmers got a nil or negative income in 2002 and another third an income lower than the minimum wage (SMIC), they got at least €0.17 per kilo whereas their Brazilian colleagues got only €0.06. That is why the poultry production of Doux in Brazil equalled its French production in 2002, and the number of workers was even larger (7,300 wage-earners and 2,800 poultry farmers as against 7,000 and 2,000 respectively). It is also why Doux closed its establishment of Briec in 2002, firing 250 wage earners and more than 100 farmers. Before Doux, the second French poultry company, Bourgoin, which employed 2,700 people in the West of France, had already gone bankrupt in October 2000. In that context, the European Commission increased the export refund from €280 per tonne of frozen chicken exported to Russia and the Middle East in January 2002 to €440 in July! So wherever you look – salaried workers, integrated farmers, European citizens, Brazilian farmers – Doux finds people to pluck.

Europe's export vocation

This idea that Europe has a vocation to export agricultural produce is an obsession to many, including those at the highest level. And France, second ranking country in the world for agricultural exports, is of course at the heart of any such idea. In a public speech to farmers in Vassy (Normandy) in December 1977, President of the Republic Valéry Giscard d'Estaing called for agriculture to become the 'green petrol of France'. This rapidly became a political slogan, reflected in the French agricultural guidance law of 1980. 'Don't call into question the export vocation of the European Union,' says President Jacques Chirac. 'Don't call into question the power and quality of French agriculture,' insisted former Prime Minister Lionel Jospin on 24 March 2001 outside the European Council in Stockholm.[15] Fortunately the new French Minister of agriculture, Hervé Gaymard, seems more reluctant to run the risk of losing the European domestic market, but has not realised how extensively the negotiating position of the European Commission for the new Agreement on Agriculture of the WTO would open the European market to other countries' exports. Jacques Chirac himself has begun to denounce the highly detrimental impact of export refunds on African farmers, but he has not yet understood that direct payments to farmers to replace export refunds have precisely the same effect.

And yet… Many received ideas do not stand up to a critical analysis of the statistics and realities of international trade. The first point to note is that primary agricultural produce makes up a constantly diminishing part of this trade.

> Agri-food products which made up 25 per cent of international trade in 1960, constitute no more than 10 per cent today. Among these products, the part made up of unprocessed agricultural produce is falling in relation to transformed products and products with a high added value.[16]

In these circumstances, why be fixated on a reduction in the price of cereals so that the EU can constantly export more on the world market? Moreover, it is the increase in solvent international demand that stimulates trade rather than a fall in tariff barriers. This we saw in the 1970s when the volume of cereals on the world market doubled in ten years (from 100 to 200 million tonnes from 1970 to 1980) without any reduction in tariff barriers. The opposite occurred in the 1980s. According to the experts, world trade in cereals should have doubled in the decade 1988–98 (increasing by 220m tonnes); in the event, it fell slightly.

Don't let us forget that the prime market for European agricultural output is the European consumer. Intra-Community exchanges of agricultural and food products (€139 billion in 2000) exceed by a long way trade with third countries (€58 billion). What is true for Europe is even more true for France: three-quarters (78.5 per cent) of its agri-food surplus is taken up by other EU member-states.

Another harsh reality for the experts in expertise: the higher the level of French exports, the more impoverished its agriculture becomes. In effect, there is an inverse relation between trends in agricultural value-added and those of agricultural surpluses. The former has fallen since 1974, the date when the first sales of agribusiness surpluses occurred, while the latter have been on the rise. In short, the farm called 'France' produces a little more and gains a little less every year. The same is true for the EU-15: if the index of agricultural net value added is taken as 100 in 1980, it had fallen to 90.8 in 1990 and to 85.0 in 1996, a decline which continues to this day. The same happened to the United Kingdom where agricultural net value added declined at current prices from £5 billion in 1989-91 to £4.4 billion in 2000, a fall of 12 per cent.[17]

In truth, everything depends on what is exported. Products with a high added value which create jobs and wealth (quality wines and cheeses, for example) bear no comparison with primary products whose added value is very low, or even negative if you deduct the subsidies. In the latter case we must recognise that without subsidies there would be no exports at all because European prices, even when subsidised, remain higher than world prices. So we should not be surprised by the miraculous increase in the European budget dedicated to arable crops by 1,000 per cent between 1984 and 1997! It rose at a rate of €1.66 billion a year to €17.5 billion in 2001. The world market, it bears repeating, is a market of surpluses. For example: with a wheat price of €119 a tonne, the net income of farming enterprises in France in 1997 was virtually zero once direct subsidies were deducted. Since the latest reduction of 15 per cent in the cereals intervention price between 2000 and 2001, the direct payment received by French wheat growers exceeds their other net income by 26 per cent! We are forced to recognise that it is only the European market, the most solvent world market, and high value-added products that are able to fuel the agrarian economy and to encourage employment.

A bewitching language of agriculture as Europe's 'green petrol' serves only to hide the huge and juicy profits that agribusiness and the large distributors have extracted from the consumers via their increased margins consequent on the severe fall of agricultural prices in Europe, margins which have enabled them to pursue their growth strategy by buying up competitors. This language also gives comfort to the agri-managers' incessant clamouring that you have to be of a certain scale to succeed on the world market. The roundabout of restructuring/concentration/industrialisation never ceases to turn, but the screeching has become so loud that many have come to realise it would be better to make it turn in the opposite direction.

2 Reforming the CAP

1992: The topsy-turvey CAP

In January 1991 Ray MacSharry, European Agricultural Commissioner announced a reform of the CAP, made unavoidable by the escalating costs of managing the surpluses. His objectives made it possible to hope for a number of significant improvements: maximising the number of farmers with a recognised dual role as both producer and custodian of the environment; redirecting subsidies to help those most in need; redistributing support in relation to the number of those economically active on each farm rather than to the amount produced; participating in rural development and in re-populating the countryside. The stakes were high, both for the farmers and for the rural world: it was a question of getting out of the impasse in which productivism had cornered them, with a concentration of activity and pollution in some places, depopulation in others. It was time to break with an expensive and unjust policy where 80 per cent of the subsidies went to 20 per cent of farmers.

On 4 February 1991, the European Commission tabled a discussion document entitled 'The Development and Future of the CAP'. It argued that

> the mechanisms of the CAP as currently applied are no longer in a position to attain certain conditions... namely, to ensure a fair standard of living for the

agricultural community, stabilise markets, ensure reasonable prices to consumers, take account of the social structure of agriculture and of the structural and natural disparities between the various agricultural regions.[1]

This document was presented to the Council of Agricultural Ministers, where it was bitterly contested over the next 14 months. Thus began a long slippage that made the resulting reform project unrecognisable, thanks to the pressure of the cereal growers and the agribusiness lobbies. In the horse trading, the proposals for the 'modulation' of subsidies paid to the large producers, specific programmes for disadvantaged regions, ceilings on output, the obligatory rotation of fallow lands – all these were abandoned. (Modulation, incidentally, is Commission-speak for capping subsides to larger farmers and using the funds released to finance other rural objectives.)

On 21 May 1992 a final agreement was signed by the Council of Agricultural Ministers of the EU-12. Intervention prices were reviewed downwards. Compensation took the form of direct payments paid to the producers, related to the number of hectares for cereals and oilseed crops (in return for taking 15 per cent of land out of production) and to the number of animals for sheep and beef farms. This system of 'decoupling' prices from costs of production aimed at getting farmers to accept the fall in domestic agricultural prices while increasing the competitiveness of their output on world markets. After 30 years of guaranteed prices for unlimited amounts – accompanied by their corollaries of massive over-production and waste of public monies – it was a total about-turn, inspired by the neoliberal credo: the total opening up of frontiers.

If the Commission's first proposals had the same objective of increased competitiveness for the EU's agri-food products, at least they wanted to use this radical shift in the

CAP to improve the income distribution among farmers and the agricultural impact on the environment. The joint pressures of the main conservative farmers' unions, agribusinesses and the member states opposed to the taxation of imported feedstuffs (the so-called rebalancing of tariffs on imported oilseeds after the lowering of tariffs on imported cereals) determined otherwise.

Setting land aside to reduce levels of production was to be a fiasco. Yields simply increased on the good fields – thanks to chemical inputs and irrigation – and the less productive fields were set aside. It was intensification here and fallow there. It was no surprise that European cereal production kept on its upward trajectory! From 1992 to 2001 the EU-15 cereal production increased by 30 million tonnes, of which 20 million tonnes were through higher yields and 10 million tons through a lower rate of set-aside than in 1993 (the first year in which it was mandatory). The generalisation of the world price as the reference point, rather than eliminating the surpluses, simply made them cheaper. The fall in cereal prices brought with it that of substitute cereal products (SCPs), encouraging the intensive production of milk and meat and consolidating the famous production system of maize/soya/concrete in dairy farming. This is the system whereby maize is grown intensively – heavily fertilised and heavily watered it can produce an output of 80–120 quintals per hectare, a third more than that of wheat grown on the same land – and is complemented with soya (imported duty-free) in its use as animal feed. On this basis animals can be kept indoors on concrete and factory farming comes into its own.

And to cap it all, maize silage falls under the same regime of public support as cereals (that is to say, subsidies that can reach €380 per hectare per year), which accentuates the disadvantage of farms that continue to use forage systems based on grasses rather than intensive monocropping of maize.

Many a day still lay ahead for the unfair distribution of subsidies, it. Gone were the modulations that would have allowed compensation for regional or structural handicaps. As someone said: 'It always rains where it's already soaking!' The CAP had changed – in order that nothing should change. And the machine for chewing up farmers was once more in motion: from 1995 to 2000 the equivalent of a million full-time workers lost their agricultural jobs, of whom 407, 000 were in Italy, 97,000 in Germany, 85,000 in France and 45,000 in the United Kingdom.

Box 2.1: Nitrogen, bacteria and the chemical industry

Leguminous plants have a wonderful property, known to peasants from time immemorial: they can fix nitrogen from the air thanks to bacteria present in their roots. More than 300 species exist in France and there are almost 7,000 species worldwide.

With cheap petroleum and the development of the chemical industry, the 'mixed cropping/livestock' system which allowed the transfer of the fertility of the meadowlands to the crops through the medium of animal manure was broken. Chemically produced nitrogen, used in ever-increasing quantities, has brought in its wake the eutrophication of numerous terrestrial, aquatic and marine environments.[2] Today, the amount of nitrogenous fertiliser used on many farms in the EU exceeds that authorised. The consumption of nitrogen fertilisers increased by 10 per cent in the EU-15 from 1992 to 1999 and by as much as 19 per cent in France. Indeed 12 of the 15 Member States have been prosecuted by the European Court of Justice under the nitrogen directive.

Only those who include leguminous plants in their crop rotation, particularly those who practice organic agriculture, manage to respect normal levels. The problem posed is that of the self-sufficiency of farm units – the ability to rely on inputs from the farm (mainly feedstuffs but also seeds, animal manure, etc.) rather than being dependent on externally sourced inputs and imported fossil fuels – and their energy efficiency. The threat is pollution of the water table and water resources generally.

Take two examples of milk production, one based on grazing cows on grass, the other based on maize. If you do a comparative study of energy inputs – both direct (fuel, electricity, gas) and indirect (fertilisers, feedstuffs, phytosanitary products, equipment) – on the one hand with energy outputs (vegetable, organic and mineral products) on the other, there is no contest. The maize-based system uses 50 per cent more energy than the grazing system. Waste? Not for everyone! Although the area devoted to leguminous plants has fallen substantially (from 6.8 million hectares in 1958 to 3.5 million today), CAP subsidies remain scandalously favourable to maize silage (€380 euros per hectare per year), a glutton when it comes to using chemical nitrogen. Yet again, public money just passes through the pocket of the farmer into the coffers of the chemical industry, while the costs of cleaning up the nitrates which have leached into the water supply are externalised, to the citizen-consumer.

The problem is widespread wherever there is intensive agriculture. In Britain it is DEFRA, the Department for Environment, Food and Rural Affairs, that is responsible for dealing with pollution problems. In 2002 it reported that 'Nitrate levels in many English waters, both ground and surface waters, are increasing', and that 'over 70 per cent of nitrate enters water from agricultural land.' Indeed, intensive agriculture is now the major source of water pollution in England; to the nitrate run-off we can add 40 per cent of all phosphates in English waters, an unknown quantity of pesticides and the majority of silt loads to English rivers and lakes which arises from heavy soil erosion from agricultural land.

The European Court of Justice has judged that Britain has

failed to meet its obligations under the 1991 Nitrates Directive to prevent and reduce agricultural nitrate pollution of waters.[3]

In Brittany, with the additional impact of factory farming, nitrate concentration in watercourses increased tenfold (from 4 to 40 mg/l) between 1970 and 1999 and 75 per cent of catchments in the department of Côtes d'Armor in 1995 were above the ceiling of 50 mg/l of nitrate. A 1999 representative poll showed that only 12.3 per cent of Bretons always drink tap water, 6 per cent often, 12.8 per cent occasionally, 15.4 per cent exceptionally and 53.5 per cent never! French households spend more than €2 billion on mineral water, six times more in real terms than in 1960.

That the CAP directly encourages polluting practices is shown by a survey of 807 farms in the Isère district that reveals a high correlation between the level of direct payments received in 1994 and 1995 and the level of nitrate pollution.

Pollution by pesticides tends to be even more harmful to health and the environment. Three quarters of Brittany's water resources are above the ceiling of 0.1µg of pesticides per litre. According to a recent investigation, 10 per cent of French fruits and vegetables presented pesticides residues and 8 per cent were above the authorised ceiling. Another survey has shown that the percentage of various food products imported into the Netherlands and presenting pesticides residues above the ceiling increased from 5 per cent in 1990 to 16 per cent in 2000.[4]

In effect, this reform of the CAP, which encouraged and indeed favoured quantity over quality, anticipated the objectives of the Uruguay Round. By adopting a system of decoupling which resembled the American model, Europe wanted to avoid facing the usual difficulties of haggling in the GATT and WTO Rounds. In the same vein, the Blair House agreement in Washington, which signalled the end of the Uruguay Round, ended by confirming Europe's dependence in the area of vegetable proteins.

We know that the bargain had been made 30 years earlier on the you-scratch-my-back-and-I'll-scratch-yours principle: to the USA went the production of vegetable proteins, to Europe that of cereals (for its own consumption). The 1973 ban, when the USA put an embargo on the export of soya following a bad harvest, brutally awakened Europe to its dependency. A protein plan was put in place in 1975, with some success, Europe moving from 19 per cent self-sufficiency in 1973 to 40 per cent at the beginning of the 1990s. But it was to be of short duration. Under attack from the USA, Europe agreed at Blair House to limit its production of oilseed plants (rape, sunflower, soya) to 5.13 million hectares. It was to build in first stagnation and then a collapse in the production of vegetable proteins. Within a few years the degree of European self-sufficiency had fallen back to 25 per cent. Thus we have reached the bizarre situation of a Europe that leaves 4 million hectares fallow and devotes another 4 million to cereals for export at low prices while importing the equivalent of 15 million hectares of vegetable proteins. Shurely shome mishtake, as *Private Eye* would have it!

The Marrakech shambles

The Blair House agreement was ratified with the signature of the Marrakech Agreements. On 15 April 1994, 134 countries gave a seven-year endorsement to what amounted to an abandonment of sovereignty on the part of these states. As their final act they agreed to set up the World Trade Organisation, with effect from 1 January 1995.

This body does not acknowledge the existence of the United Nations as an institution. In practice, this means that the WTO is bound neither by the UN Charter, nor by its Declaration of Universal Rights, nor by the International

Covenant on Economic, Social and Cultural Rights of 1966 ratified by 141 States, nor by the International Covenant on Civil and Political Rights of the same year ratified by 95 States.

The Agreement on Agriculture (AoA) starts from the basic premise that over the course of time the member states of the WTO have put health, social and environmental regulations in place at a national level that are more constraining than need be. According to the WTO, the hidden objective of such rules has been to protect local producers insidiously against competition from other countries. As from 1 January 1995, therefore, member states had to make an inventory of their protective measures, evaluate the obstacles these created to the liberalisation of international trade and translate them into visible and quantifiable customs duties or tariffs (the so-called process of tariffication). Over time these tariffs must be reduced significantly (by 36 per cent).

> The consequences of such a dismantling are easy to imagine. When Argentinean beef enters Europe at €1.07 per kilo (as against a producer price that has fluctuated between €2.5 and €3.1 in France in the last four years), pork at 30 cents (as against a producer price that has fluctuated between €1.2 and €2.0 in France in the last four years) and maize at €67 per tonne (it has not been lower than €100 in France in the last two years, a level that corresponds to the reduced intervention price in operation since July 2001), the large distributors and agribusiness can put pressure on European farmers to meet these new price levels.[5]

At the same time, countries must reduce the volume of their subsidised exports (by 21 per cent for rich countries and 13.3 per cent for poor countries) and the value of the corresponding subsidies (by 36 per cent for rich countries and 24 per cent for poor countries). In addition, according to the 'minimum access' clause, they must open up their domestic agri-food market, with a maximum tariff of two-thirds of the normal tariff, for at least 4 per cent of domestic consumption in poor countries and 5 per cent in rich countries. And this is mandatory for all agri-food products even when countries are self-sufficient in a given agri-food item, and even if the tariff-quotas so opened are not necessarily fulfilled if the private importing companies are not interested.

The immediate effect of this opening of frontiers was to put the subsistence crops of Southern countries in danger. Thus South Korea and the Philippines, for example, countries that were self-sufficient in rice, were none the less obliged to allow the import of inferior quality rice. This rice, arriving at a cheaper price than local produce, called into question the food self-sufficiency of these countries, forced farmers out of business and exacerbated the rural exodus.

Box 2.2: The effects of trade liberalisation

A survey for a group of Swedish NGOs covering 27 case studies and experiences of the effects of trade liberalisation (the removal or reduction of barriers to international trade in goods and services) on food security and poverty was published in 2002. It reported that:

On the key question of what trade liberalisation has done to people who are already food insecure, their evidence appears remarkably consistent. The common and overriding message can be summed up in a sentence from Hezron Nyangito's study of Kenya: 'liberalised trade, including WTO trade agreements, benefits only the rich while the majority of the poor do not benefit but are instead made more vulnerable to food insecurity.'[6]

The effects of trade liberalisation are felt at many levels. In societies where the majority of people belong to farming families, cheap imports – often at dumping prices – have an immediate, detrimental effect on millions of producers. Farmers producing for local markets are often forced out of business and governments give local food production less priority while increasing the priority they accord to crops for export. Even where additional revenue is earned, most of it is captured by traders and large transnational companies, not the farmers who produce the export crops. In addition, this export orientation brings other costs: increased use of fertilisers and pesticides (often imported), depletion of water resources that had previously been used for growing local food crops, and increasing pollution.

Women, who produce 60 to 75 per cent of food in most African countries, have been particularly affected by the elimination of government subsidies, the drying up of credit and the surge of food imports as a result of trade liberalisation.

It is hard to know how many people have lost their jobs as a result of liberalisation but a study of Mexico shows that 15 per cent of the economically active population in agriculture – between 700,000 and 800,000 people – have been forced into the ranks of the unemployed by reduced maize prices. (See Box 4.1)

Under US pressure, the fundamental aims in these negotiations remained unchanged: to ease access to markets for foreign products and to reduce state support to farmers. In moving towards this, the WTO set up a hierarchy among subsidies, from those judged to be protectionist to those having little or no distorting effect on international markets. Thus the AoA distinguishes, in descending order of protectionist effects, the so-called red, amber, and green 'boxes', based on traffic light principles. At a late stage of the negotiations, largely to get a compromise with the EU, a blue 'box' was added.

The first, the *red* box, is generally considered to be empty since it contains only forms of support outlawed under the AoA (such as variable levies and import quotas), but the Food and Agriculture Organisation of the United Nations (FAO) and some authors put border supports (tariffs and export subsidies) into it. This is more appropriate since these supports are subject to a much higher reduction (36 per cent) than domestic coupled supports (20 per cent), which implies that they are considered more protectionist. International negotiations stumbled particularly on the contents of this box. Europe, under pressure from agribusiness, refused to simply abandon those measures that allowed it to pour its surpluses (whether of pork, poultry, milk or cereals) on to the world market.

In the *amber* box we find domestic supports said to be 'coupled', that is, linked to production or prices, and thus considered protectionist. These are to be abandoned in the longer run, but are allowed for the time being so long as they are gradually reduced. Supports aiming to keep domestic prices at higher levels than they would otherwise be form part of this category of support. They include such things as regulation of market prices through guaranteed prices, government intervention and the like, plus some forms of direct payment such as input or investment subsidies.

The *green* box groups together those supports that are fully decoupled (said to have no effect on agricultural production), such as agro-environmental supports, aid to disadvantaged regions, income guarantees or public research. They are not subject to reductions and can even increase.

The anomalous *blue* box brings together measures that one might have expected to find in the amber box but were allowed to continue for nine years (up to December 2003) without commitment to their reduction. These are supports that are in part decoupled from production and which are said not to give direct encouragement to the producer to increase levels of production. Since the US Farm Bill of 1996 and the disappearance of the deficiency payments linked to target prices in the US, CAP direct payments per hectare or per head of cattle possessed by EU farmers in the base years 1989–91 have been the main items featuring in this category.

For the WTO, all support systems must in the end be modified to fall entirely in the green box. But this game of boxes is in effect a con, one way of dressing up supports which are rapidly rising.[7] Thus, green supports of the 24 OECD member countries rose from $54 billion in 1986–88 to $120 billion in 1996 (the delay of several countries in notifying supports to the WTO does not allow for more up-to-date figures) and the European Union's blue box (which accounts for more than 90 per cent of the world's total in that box) did not exist before 1993 but reached $27.4 billion in 2001. Whereas the OECD's total domestic supports remained stable ($234 billion in 1986–88, $232 billion in 1997), export subsidies from the European Union in the same period – which account for 90 per cent of all export subsidies notified by 25 countries to the WTO – declined from $11.4 billion in 1986–88 to $4.8 billion in 1998 to $3.4 billion in 2001. Of course, decoupled or not, this differentiation among supports according to coloured boxes is totally mystifying. They all allow production and exporting at below full production costs and consequently have the same dumping effect as export subsidies when the products that benefit are exported. This is highly detrimental to poor countries that are incapable of supporting their agriculture in this way especially since they are also denied the right to maintain high tariffs.

As Article 20 of the AoA reminds us we are truly facing a process of illusory liberalisation of agricultural trade. This article gave a nod of recognition towards the weaknesses of the current agreement by stating that the ongoing negotiations should take into account 'non-trade concerns, special and differential treatment to developing country Members, and the objective to establish a fair and market-oriented agricultural trading system'. Agricultural employment, nowhere mentioned, is the great loser since the actual programme of structural adjustment put in place leads directly to the concentration of production, encouraged of course in the EU by CAP subsidies.

This liberalisation is illusory since, if agricultural income is more and more decoupled from production, direct supports come to compensate for the reduction in tariff duties. What lurks behind this façade is nothing less than an exacerbation of the inequalities between rich and poor countries: it is simple for poor countries to install customs tariffs, but the mechanism of direct support is an option available only to countries with significant budgetary resources. Moreover, since agricultural products circulate at false prices, the internal coherence of agriculture, like its articulation with the rest of the economy, can be compromised. Thus we have increased specialisation of farms and regions, development of factory farm production and an associated decline of meadow and pasturelands, the consequence of the importation of concentrated feeds at cheap prices.

'Do as I say, not as I do.' The duplicity is evident in the confrontation between the EU and the USA, each bloc authorised to support its agriculture in substantial ways. The OECD has noted that public supports for agriculture, far from declining, are exploding exponentially.

American agricultural policy for the period 1996–2000 is a good case in point (see Box 5.1). The so-called FAIR Act (Federal Agricultural Improvement and Reform) passed by Congress in 1996 saw itself initiating a new agricultural politics. It turned out to be a disaster; and Congress had repeatedly to authorise emergency measures of crisis aid, fiscal relief and massive intervention purchases. In 1999, American farmers received a record level of direct support: more than $20 billion as against a mere $7.5 billion in 1997. Finally, these annual emergency relief measures were replaced by the Farm Security and Rural Investment Act in May 2002. This provides for a staggering $18 billion a year on agricultural support over the next ten years – generally 'decoupled' and therefore legitimate in WTO terms. None of it looks like a good advert for liberalisation!

Box 2.3: When fewer (farms) means more (produced)

Concentration, concentration is the watchword that summarises 40 years in the fruit and vegetable sectors. Production, distribution, marketing – nothing has escaped from the phenomenon under way in the wake of the development of an ever more powerful, large-scale mass marketing. In 1999 the Carrefour-Promodes merger pushed this group into number one in Europe and number two in the world of distribution. It controlled 5,424 shops directly at the end of September 2002, of which 688 were hypermarkets, 1,432 supermarkets and 3,050 maxi-discounts in 30 countries – for a turnover before tax of €69.5 billion in 2001 (€82 billion if you take into account an additional 4,000 or so franchised shops) and a net profit of €1.2 billion, with 383,000 employees. Faced with this mastodon, the liberal credo has a simple response: the producers must organise – but there are fewer and fewer producers marketing an ever-increasing output. From concentration of marketing we slip rapidly into a concentration of production encouraged by the absence of any limits to the size of production units or investment subsidies.

Take the example of the Département du Nord in France, where this is as true for apples or tomatoes as it is for endives. There, five producers, representing 20 per cent of the output of 800 farmers belonging to seven co-ops, formed their own producers' organisation. It was worth doing since under the new Common Market regime their turnover of more than €3 million entitled them to official subsidies for producer organisations. The result of all this: within ten years the 5,000 producers of endives had melted away like snow. No more than 1,200 remained. That is the point: public monies finance both concentration and the squeezing out of small farmers.

More generally, the European Union of the 15 lost almost half its full-time equivalent agricultural employment in the period 1980–2001 (employment falling from 11.8 million to 6 million). Of this loss, 2.1 million has been since 1990 (300,000 of it in France). At the same time, the average agricultural area per holding increased in the EU-12 from 15 to 18.2 hectares (1990–97) but from 30.5 to 41.7 hectares in France. In France, the number of farmers receiving direct payments for cereals, pulses and oilseeds, dropped by 100,000 between 1993 (459,000) and 2001 (358,000). The number of French farms raising cattle has been reduced by a factor of 3.9 between 1970 (1,052,000) and 2000 (268,000); those raising dairy cows have fallen even more spectacularly, by a factor of 6.2 (from 815,000 to 131,000). The number of French farms rearing pigs declined by 42 per cent from 1988 to 2000, whereas the number of those rearing more than 1,000 pigs in concentrated conditions is now two-thirds of all production as against one-third in 1988. During the same period, the number of sheep farmers also declined by 42 per cent.

1999: from Berlin to Seattle

In March 1999, the 15 Ministers of Agriculture meeting in Berlin huddled over a new CAP reform, integrated into a series of propositions called Agenda 2000.[8] The objective was to prepare the European countries for new WTO negotiations and for enlargement of the Union to the countries of central and eastern Europe (the CEECs). There was nothing particularly new on the agenda: the eternal refrain was once again that the competitiveness of European agriculture must be improved without respite in order to maintain its presence in the world markets. The one real change has been the creation of the 'second pillar' of the CAP, that of rural development, in order to support the 'non-commercial aspects of agriculture' more effectively; in a word the famous multifunctionality about which so much has been said. (This is the recognition that the farmer has many roles; not just food producer but guardian of the environment and the rural landscape as well.)[9] For all that, there were no surprises: totally in keeping with the 1992 reform, intervention prices were lowered – 15 per cent for arable crops and 20 per cent for beef – and this fall was compensated by a rise in direct supports. Even if certain products escaped this reform – milk, sugar, fruit and vegetables, poultry – the logic is always that of aligning European prices with world prices in order to be able to export without export subsidies (restitutions). This logic of always giving more money to compensate for losses makes the CAP ever more expensive. So, for example, on its cereal account the Guarantee Fund saw a rise from €1.65 billion in 1984 to €12 billion in 1995, an increase of 720 per cent!

Despite all this, the results for most farmers have not been at all favourable. The fall in the intervention price translates into a reality that is hard to bear. Little by little, the EU and the WTO have removed all self-sufficiency from cereal, beef and sheep producers. Direct supports exceed net income in every case: 125 per cent of the net income of an average grain producer, 129 per cent of that of a cattle farmer, 140 per cent of a sheep farmer! Put another way, when a producer spends €16 (that is the average outlay in France) to produce a quintal (hundredweight) of cereal, the sale of the product only brings back €10.7 and the direct supports another €4.7 to €5.3. What other profession would accept such a situation? Worse still, the fall in agricultural prices decided on in 1999 has only been partially compensated for in increased support. The message is clear: to maintain their income, the EU is asking those farmers who manage to remain in farming to work harder: that is to say, both to expand and to intensify their production! What salaried workers would accept an increase of 10 per cent in working time in order to maintain their salary – and even more to get any increase?

Beyond the budgetary costs of such a policy, the fact of producing at a very low price allows no constraints in the process of production (hence the incessant pressure to use hormones, GMOs, animal feedstuffs;[10] and hence, too, no limits on the size of production units, or ceilings on support levels). Following all this is the inevitability of further disastrous consequences whether with regard to employment levels, the environment, biodiversity or food quality. The affirmation of the 'export vocation' as the central axis of the CAP, in 1999 as in 1992, continues to subordinate the farmer to the free market chopping block.

Box 2.4: Dirty hands on seeds

The offensive is now general, the hold-up envisaged on a planetary level. The lobbies are at work everywhere and nothing escapes their appetite for domination. The stakes? Nothing less than the control of life itself. Plants have an extraordinary property, shocking in the eyes of the seed lobby: they reproduce by themselves. Over millennia, humankind has selected and cultivated those plants best adapted to particular localities and climates as well as to their needs and tastes. Reproducing and selecting seeds themselves, small farmers have been the guardians of genetic diversity, the real heritage of humanity.

At the beginning of the 1970s, however, the idea of transforming the seed market into a captive market was born. It was a question of forcing farmers to repurchase new seed each year, whether through the use of regulatory constraints or technological ones (F1 hybrids, then genetically modified seeds). From 1978 the International Union for the Protection of New Varieties of Plants (UPOV) decreed that farm seed was a 'farmer's privilege'. In 1991 it decided that this privilege was henceforth optional, being considered as a 'derogation of the rights of the plant breeder'.

The result: farmers can continue their millennia-long practice on condition that they pay a copyright fee: a tax on farm-saved seed. Given this logic, the 1994 European directive surprised no one: 'Member states can, if they wish, make the receiving of CAP subsidies subject to the use of certified seed.' And in 1997 the Agricultural Council of Ministers made the purchase of certified seed obligatory for hard wheat – without any justification in terms of output or quality. So one part of the CAP subsidy merely passes through the farmer to finish in the pocket of the seed producer. And they talk of diversion of funds!

This agri-exporting model is presented as the only valid one, particularly in relation to the countries of central and eastern Europe (CEECs), whose farmer/peasant populations can already foresee the high price they will be called on to pay for their integration into the European Union. The CAP and the opening of their markets, corollaries of entry into the EU, will rapidly destroy what 40 years of communism, however destructive, failed to do: Polish agriculture and its 2 million farmers. The verdict on them has been decided in advance: they are not competitive. In the case of the CEECs generally, the 'retraining' of millions of farmers, in countries where unemployment levels are very high (13 per cent of the economically active in

Poland, and up to 20 per cent in some of its regions) is the chief concern of European managers. In these countries, where agriculture has remained important, they want to impose an immediate dismantling. European negotiators and the governments of the candidate countries envisage the disappearance of no less than 45 per cent of farm units. The case of the CEECs applies more generally; the conquest of the world market signifies the end of the farmer.

Is this an unavoidable march to the precipice? The end of 1999 saw a shot across the bows of what is a suicidal strategy for society as a whole. That was Seattle and the failure of the WTO intergovernmental conferences. The launching of the Millennium Round was a resounding flop, thanks to the dual mobilisation of a new social movement and of the developing countries, determined to make their voices heard centre stage. The former gave expression to the spectacular eruption of civil society into the political arena. Forcefully rejecting the idea that reference to the world market should serve as the standard for determining the fate of millions of farmers, the counter-summit exposed and denounced the alignment of the EU with the WTO in relation to agriculture. From now on, it was clear that to change the CAP fundamentally, the Agreement on Agriculture would also have to be changed – and vice versa. The perverse effects of subsidies on exports cannot be eliminated by another cosmetic rearrangement, under cover of words like multifunctionality or decoupling. As for the poor countries, grouped together in the G77, they no longer intended to play the role of eternal victims of international negotiations. As the delegate from Mauritius put it, loud and clear: 'Developing countries have lost everything in this negotiation, but we are expected put our heads on the chopping block with dignity.' They won't do so any longer.

Headlong to disaster!

'It is a matter of continuing to liberalise and to extend the markets for agricultural goods in order to contribute to sustained economic growth.' Such is the mandate given by the EU to Pascal Lamy, the Commissioner responsible for Trade at the WTO with regard to agricultural questions. 'Master globalisation', 'multifunctionality', 'be open to the demands of developing countries', 'commercial opening up' – no key phrase is missing from the repeated refrain.

After Seattle, the EU and the USA understood that they needed the support of the developing countries and searched for new ideas in order to attract their support.

At Doha (Qatar) an intense frenzy reigned in the preparations for the ministerial conference scheduled for November 2001. The EU declared itself prepared to negotiate a new reduction in export subsidies so long as all forms of support for exports of agricultural and food products were put on the same footing. Food aid was particularly targeted and fingers pointed at the USA, which uses such aid more to manage its surpluses or to develop commercial outlets than to respond to peoples' needs. In relation to the developing countries, the EU announced an initiative called 'Everything but Arms'. This was approved by the European Council of Trade Ministers and came into effect from 5 March 2002.

The seduction offensive aimed at the poorest countries in the world, hypocritically rebaptised as the 'Least Developed Countries', consisted of allowing all their products (excepting arms and munitions) access to the European market without taxes or quotas.. In a ferociously competitive market jungle such generosity arouses doubts. And a closer examination shows that the gift is poisoned![11]

For three 'key' products benefiting from special treatment – rice, sugar and bananas – the opening of the European market was deferred, to sometime between 2002 and 2009. In the meantime, the poor countries were asked to support the European proposals in the current WTO negotiations! But there was worse: the European initiative threw overboard the mechanisms of the agreements with the ACP (African, Caribbean, and Pacific Ocean) countries previously made at Yaoundé, Lomé and Cotonou. According to these agreements, the producers in these countries benefited from a certain, restricted access to the European market, but at price levels above those of the world market. Henceforth, Europe proposed to open its markets to ACP produce – but at world market prices!

Who would be the losers? Farmers confronted with a collapse in prices without any mechanism to control supply; the poorest countries exhorted to privilege export crops to the detriment of subsistence agriculture and forced to satisfy their internal food needs by importing at world market prices; European farmers who would see their incomes reduced. Who the winners? The transnationals specialising in international exchange, whether in trade, processing, banking or insurance. The Doha Agreement, concluded on 10 November within the framework of the WTO which allowed for the relaunching of international negotiations favouring the liberalisation of the economy, reinforced this tendency. Everything is ready for a return to colonialism with a new look. Unless, with grain after grain of sand, the wheels jam.[12]

3 French agricultural trade unionism: the long march of the Confédération Paysanne

The history of agricultural trade unionism in France is unique. A brief account of it will go some way to explaining why the Confédération Paysanne made such a spectacular entry onto the national and the international scene in 1999 with the symbolic dismantling of a McDonald's outlet then being built in the French town of Millau in the heart of Roquefort country. (See Box 3.1.)

For many, the very existence of the Confédération was a surprise. But different currents were at work in the depths of the French countryside long before any waves appeared to trouble the apparently smooth surface of the farming world. Critical analyses of the effects of the new Common Agricultural Policy first began to appear towards the end of the 1960s. As part of this critique, the myth of farmers' unity was called into question. So too was the increasingly important place of large-scale economic organisations (both private and cooperative) in the world of agriculture.

The FNSEA (the National Federation of Farmers' Unions)

The myth of farmers' unity was extremely useful for assuring the domination of a 'Soviet-style' agricultural trade union in France, the FNSEA (Fédération nationale des syndicats d'exploitants agricoles or National Federation of Farmers' Unions).[1] A real example of 'French exceptionalism', it is worth a closer look. For if the CAP lies at the foundation of the greatest plan for structural adjustment ever imposed on the agricultural world in Europe, it would never have been so effective without the enormous, determined and continuous support of a union claiming to defend – against all the evidence – the supposedly common interests of small farmers and agri-managers alike.

The FNSEA was created in 1946 out of the ruins of the Corporation paysanne, the farmers' corporation which the Vichy regime had established. Much of the spirit of the former was, however, maintained. The 'unity of all farmers' was solemnly proclaimed by FNSEA's first president Eugène Forget on 12 March 1946 and, until the Mitterrand government changed things in the 1980s, the FNSEA was by law the only recognised farmers' union. All farmers, independent of their status – whether small farmers, landowners, renters, or integrated producers – belonged to the single union.

When de Gaulle's Fifth Republic opted for the most rapid possible modernisation of agriculture, the union, by this time controlled by the large grain barons, was ready. As the CAP evolved, the corporate picture of a united farming community facing the rest of society was maintained. The FNSEA came to share responsibility for farm policy with the Ministry of Agriculture, negotiating in secret behind the back of the French National Assembly.

'Controlling the quasi-totality of organisations in the field [of agriculture] with an iron fist, dictating its wishes to ministers, benefiting from the manna of public funds,' the FNSEA and its 'youth' section, the Centre nationale des jeunes agriculteurs (CNJA – National Centre for Young Farmers), came to regard farmers as 'modern' business managers.[2] They developed a monolithic view of the right way to farm, a view ruthlessly imposed over the decades. Writing in the early 1960s, the American academic Gordon Wright already noted that: 'The arguments of the FNSEA's critics are perhaps more convincing than those of its defenders. … Whether for selfish reasons or not, the FNSEA leaders focused their main lobbying efforts on goals that would benefit the large growers more directly than the small peasants,' (widening the gap between what was coming to be called 'France's two agricultures' in the 1950s).[3]

For the FNSEA leaders the notion of the small farmer, captured in the traditional meanings of the word *paysan*, was quite retrograde. The very word *paysan* took on a perjorative hue; they were very definitely '*exploitants*' not '*paysans*'. Those who have a different conception of the profession of farming had better watch out if they are tempted to stray from a super-scientific model in which the constant reference to 'modernity' has taken the form, disastrous and symbolic at the same time, of defending the use of animal feedstuffs (see Chapter 2, note 9)! Those wanting to convert to organic agriculture, for instance, have been given a very hard time of it. As one farmer explains:

> It was *the* trade union, a powerful machine that controlled every sector – from meat to milk passing through fruit and vegetables. At the smallest difficulty, it could always produce a specialist. In the countryside no one would conceive of not being a member. The force of habit is very strong.[4]

It is this force of habit, however, that a new trade-union intervention was to shake, year by year, struggle after struggle. In challenging the single union, it was also faced with the huge 'extended family' of interlinked organisations which had come to dominate all aspects of the agricultural world: not just the FNSEA and the CNJA but also the permanent assembly of Chambers of Agriculture, the social insurance scheme for farmers run by the MSA, the farmers' insurance company Groupama, the Crédit Agricole bank (the largest European bank today), the SAFER, responsible for the distribution of farming land that falls vacant and ensuring that it continues to be farmed, the cooperatives and a variety of other institutions including advice, training and promotional centres. The partnership of the state and the single union, sharing the same project of a productivist and industrialised agriculture, was to enter increasingly turbulent times.

The rumblings of opposition

In 1969, a group of like-minded people around Bernard Lambert within France's Western region of farmers' unions had been reflecting on the effects of the CAP and challenged Sicco Mansholt about its impact on small farmers in peripheral regions of Europe. Influenced by the events of 1968, Lambert published his book *Paysans et la lutte de classes* (Farmers and the Class Struggle) in April 1970. His use of the word *paysans* was a quite deliberate exercise in recuperating the notion of a farmer attached organically to the land as opposed to that of agri-manager. At much the same time, an oppositional current grouped around Lambert in the CNJA and began publishing a journal, *Vent de l'ouest* (West Wind), at the end of 1970. A new conception was arising, opposed to the dominant discourse of farmers as 'enterprise chiefs': that of the 'worker farmer'. The latter no longer demanded remuneration for their work from the state but from the firms that creamed off the added value they produced.

The milk strike in 1972, born out of a disagreement between the directors of the private dairies and those running the co-ops about a milk price that had been lowered, marked the emergence of this current. It was soon to organise its first national rallies.

This new current turned its attentions beyond the burgeoning agri-food industry to include the banks and landed property owners. Farmers were increasingly integrated into the agri-food industry. What integration meant was that the farmer took the financial risk of investing in buildings for intensive poultry farming, say, while the firms signed an 'integration contact' in which they undertook to supply young chicks, feedstuffs and so on and to buy the mature birds. But when firms decided they didn't need the poultry they proceeded to leave the hen houses empty (on health grounds!) for what could be extended periods, leaving the farmers to service the loans they had taken out to pay for the buildings in the first place. Tired of shouldering the risks of investing and of stock rearing, while those doing the integrating pocketed the benefits, many farmers took on and won cases against the agri-food industry.

More or less everywhere, the watchword was opposition to the 'cumulards' (non-agriculturists who had been buying up whole chains of farms in order to operate them with hired labour), gathering together everyone who believed any available land should go to those who needed it most. (Many young farmers especially in the west found themselves exclude from access to farming because of the purchases of the 'cumulards', who proceeded to evict many long-standing tenant farmers.[3]) Thanks also to very strong union actions against the Crédit agricole (including bank occupations etc.)

others, though strangled by debt, managed to hang onto their farms (i.e. their 'tools of production') and to remain in farming.

While all these grassroots struggles were taking place, the critique of the productivist model, given a boost by the CAP and the agricultural guidance laws, was being deepened. The resistance to the disappearance of farmers was to show itself with a bang on the limestone hills of the Larzac at the south end of the Massif central in South West France. It really was a matter of a contest between the dominant mode of production and the quest for an altogether new agricultural approach, one that was integrated into a perspective of social reconstruction.

The Larzac dispute provided a crucible for a new approach. The immediate threat was not the CAP but the army, which wished to extend its military camp there. An anti-military network explored ways of helping local farmers to oppose this extension (and drew in a young student drop-out and conscientious objector from Bordeaux, José Bové, who had become active in non-violent libertarian networks). The movement was helped, too, by the fast of Lanzo del Vasto, often called Mahatma Gandhi's 'first disciple in the West' and spiritual leader of the Arche Community which lay in the foothills of the Larzac. At Easter 1972 he embarked on a 15-day fast which provided the catalyst for 103 farmers to come together and take an oath never to sell their farms to the army. A prolonged struggle took place as they were threatened with eviction and defended by supporters from all over France, as this struggle drew support from very diverse sources, including workers from the occupied Lip watch factory, feminist activists, teachers, academics, much of the far left and, not least, Lambert's Worker-Farmers' movement. An ongoing war of manoeuvre took place. By winter 1975 the farmers on the plateau had decided to try to occupy firms bought up by the army and left vacant to deteriorate. Bové and his wife Alice were among those who moved in and became a permanent part of the struggle.

The farming community, while generally radical, was not united and was to split in 1981 when the main farmers' unions, grouped in the CDJA (the Departmental Young Farmers' Union), suddenly voted to allow a small extension to the military camp. The radicals walked out of the union. A few months later François Mitterrand won the presidential election and immediately fulfilled some of his election promises. The proposed nuclear power station at Plogoff was cancelled, as was the proposed extension to the army camp on the Larzac.

In 1981, too, trade-union pluralism was recognised, the Confédération national des syndicates de travailleurs paysans (CNSTP – National Confederation of Unions of Worker Farmers) was born, regrouping the Farmer-Workers and a certain number of trade-union groups and departmental committees. The Larzac radicals who had left the CDJA were drawn in. The calling into question of productivism was decisive in the unification of the movement, brought together in its first national meetings in March 1982. The early 1980s saw things really being shaken up. On the Larzac, a collectively owned association (under the name Société civile des terres de Larzac or SCTL) was created to manage the 6,300 hectares liberated by the abandonment of the project to extend the military camp. It was granted a long lease by the state and Bernard Lambert, spokesperson of the CNSTP, could declare: 'This will be the laboratory for new forms of land management in France.' And it was just that.

In 1982, as part of the process of developing alternatives to the single union, another organisation emerged: the Fédération nationale des syndicates paysans (FNSP). This was set up out of non-aligned departmental CDJAs and departmental FDSEAs excluded in the course of internal and minority struggles within the heart of the FNSEA against its practice of co-management with the state and against the iron hand of the cereal and beet producers over the professional organisations.

In November 1982, it had its first congress in Paris on the theme of a 'guaranteed minimum income for all farmers'. A year later, ten years after the first important assembly on the Larzac, the CNSTP held a congress at Millau with 'small farmer status' on the agenda.

The birth of the Confédération

In May 1986 when the number of farmers in difficulty was growing and the intensification of production and enlargement of existing farms was blocking the installation of young farmers, the FNSP and the CNSTP launched a series of Small Farmers' Hearings (*assises paysannes*). The whole of the following winter, at meetings organised in villages, cantons and departments, thousands and thousands of farmers debated amongst themselves, but also with locally elected representatives, with teachers and researchers. On the 17 and 18 March 1987, at Bondy, 500 delegates from 70 departments drew the conclusions from this immense ferment of ideas, anguishes and hopes. Out of the downward spiral of the CAP and the impasse of industrial agriculture, the need for a new agriculture which could support its workers, be respectful of the land and the environment and cover the whole of the country, the project of a 'small farmers' agriculture' (*l'agriculture paysanne*) was born (see Appendix 1). Forty days later, a new trade-union organisation entered the arena as bearer of this project: this was the Confédération Paysanne.

There was just time to organise a first congress and, in February 1988, 70 departments converged on Paris in a long march for fair remuneration for farmers' labour. The following year, more than 1,000 farmers accompanied by 500 elected rural representatives, demonstrated again at Paris, for the survival of the rural milieu. Its slogan 'No country(side) without farmers' loses something in translation but the original, '*Pas de pays sans paysans*' quickly became famous.

National initiatives succeeded one another in a sustained rhythm. In 1990 the colloquium 'Agriculture in Difficulty Speaks Out' prefigured the birth of the national association Solidarité Paysan (Farmers' Solidarity) which rapidly put down roots in dozens of departments. Then came 'Farms of the Future' which alerted the public at large to the Confédération's proposals. These were high points of an ongoing struggle and wouldn't have existed without thousands of actions, large and small, whether they created waves or remained barely known, which affirmed, day after day, the presence of the Confédération Paysanne on the ground. Round after round of elections to the Chambers of Agriculture consolidated and embedded these developments: 13 per cent of the votes in 1983 (for the CNSTP and the FNSP), 18 per cent in 1989, 20.6 per cent in 1995 and 27.8 per cent in 2001.

In parallel, the Confédération Paysanne involved itself more and more firmly in that critical current which was vigorous in its opposition to developments in international negotiations. So in spring 1991, when the European Union was in the process of reforming the CAP, the Confédération Paysanne and the Coordination Paysanne Européene (which the Confédération Paysanne had contributed to creating in 1986, and of which it is a member) argued forcefully for a different division of public funds and of crops, in order to maintain the number of farmers. Important actions succeeded one another, including an occupation of the New Zealand embassy to denounce the massive lamb imports, and a battle against a gigantic battery chicken farm set up in the Marne by Pohlmann, a German industrial egg producer.

The Confédération Paysanne also participated, with the Coordination Paysanne Européene in the creation of Via Campesina in 1992. This is an international farmers' movement which rapidly enrolled around 100 farmers' organisations from almost 70 countries, largely from the South. That same year, in December, Confédération Paysanne was present in Geneva where almost 10,000 demonstrators marched behind the banner: 'Act for an alternative to the GATT'. The permanent deepening of its understanding led it naturally to take up responsibilities at the heart of ATTAC (the French movement for democratic control of financial markets and thier institutions) when it was created in 1998.

And then there was a certain 12 August 1999 and the (very partial) dismantling of McDonald's at Millau. This symbolic action fitted perfectly within the historic culture of confrontation shared among those who took part and had a high added value. Recall the definition which the Confédération Paysanne had given to legitimise its own existence: it was a trade union 'for a small farmers' agriculture and the defence of its workers'. If the second term implied actions of resistance, both individual and collective, and the need for concrete action against the elimination of small farmers and for the improvement of their living conditions, the first referred naturally to a project which had to provide answers to the fundamental questions which society poses about agriculture, food and the environment.

Box 3.1: The McDonald's action and its aftermath

On 12 August 1999 the Confédération Paysanne and a local Union of Sheepmilk Producers called a rally outside a McDonald's outlet then being constructed just outside the town of Millau in the Aveyron. It was in response to a United States decision to impose a punitive 100 per cent surtax on a variety of European Union exports, in retaliation against the

EU ban on the import of US meat from animals treated with BST growth hormone. Notable among the products selected for surcharge was the local speciality, Roquefort cheese.

The préfet was notified in advance, the demonstration was publicised and 300 demonstrators turned out, half from the town, half from the surrounding farms. The police had been told that the intention was to dismantle the McDonald's and offered to get the firm to supply a symbolic billboard for demolition, an offer courteously refused! The demonstrators – men, women, children – duly began to take the flimsy structure apart, removing roof panels, fuseboxes, partitions and the like. These were loaded on to carts and paraded through the town, cheered by the local population, before being unloaded outside the prefecture.

The wrath of the established order was not long in falling. The media presented the event as a 'ransacking'; the manager of the McDonald's claimed a million francs (around €150,000) damage, and the préfet stated that the demonstrators had hidden behind children to avoid police intervention! A warrant was issued for the arrest of five farmers – Raymond Fabrègues, Léon Maillé, Christian Roqueirol, Jean-Emile Sanchez and José Bové – as well as that of the President of the federation of local groups in the area, Jacques Barthélémy. Amid a large police presence those arrested (all except Bové who had already gone on holiday) were hauled off to the police station and hearings held there on the grounds that it was 'too dangerous' to take them down the road to the local courthouse! Finally they were remanded, accused of conspiracy to cause criminal damage. Bové turned himself in a few days later after giving a press conference, and was also remanded. Barthélémy was released the same day and punitive bail conditions (around £10,000 each) imposed by an over-zealous magistrate on the others. The Confédération Paysanne stumped up bail for the farmers, but Bové refused it, deciding to sit it out in prison.

The magistrate's attempt to crush the union and the opposition it incarnated backfired spectacularly as support for those arrested grew; a photo of Bové in handcuffs as he was led to the courts consolidated his celebrity. (The contrast between their treatment and the lack of action against those FNSEA farmers who had ransacked the offices of the then-Environment Minister Dominique Voynet less than two years previously was not lost on people.) Even before a defence fund was set up, small donations began to flow in from around the world; eventually some £70,000 was received.

The action was an astonishing success in linking together themes which had previously been isolated. Concerns about the quality of food (hormone-fed beef, genetically modified organisms, Belgian chickens contaminated with dioxin) were linked to unease about the growing liberalisation of world trade and the right to protest freely. Bové, increasingly seen popularly as a political prisoner and in no way a criminal, was released eventually after 19 days in gaol.

Following their release, François Dufour of the Confédération Paysanne and his colleagues argued the case unceasingly in a series of nation-wide meetings, speeches and interviews, culminating in a two-day festival of support at the small town of Millau on 1–2 July 2000 when the case finally came to trial. To the chagrin of its conservative mayor, a staggering 100,000 people attended.

The trial was indeed a political trial, but the real accused were not the ten farmers finally charged, but the process of liberal globalisation itself, put in the dock by an astonishing, ebullient and internationalist French social movement which had succeeded in uniting support across widely divergent sectors of society.

At the trial the exaggerated accusations of the prosecution case were naturally enough disputed (were, for example, the electric cables 'torn out' or 'removed'), nicely summed up by accused Alain Soulié's cheerful: 'Let us say that there was a festive dismantling accompanied by collateral damage!' A small amount of damage was acknowledged as in the nature of things, but neither damage nor destruction for its own sake. Most importantly, the police accusation that Bové had threatened to return to McDonald's, next time with a bomb, was totally discredited. Even the prosecutor recognised that 'the whole world seems to approve of last summer's action against McDonald's' and was reduced to arguing that legitimacy does not make for legality.

The core of the defence was 100 per cent political. Seventeen activists from the 'global social movement' were called to give evidence about the effects of liberal globalisation around the world, including farmers' movement representatives like Bill Christison from the National Family Farm Coalition in the USA, Rafael Alegria general secretary of Via Campesina, Rafael Mariano from the Philippines and Mamadou Cissoko from Senegal. Also testifying about the effects of liberal globalisation were well-known activists like Vandana Shiva from India, Lori Wallach from 'Public Citizen' in the USA and Susan George from France and trade unionists like Louis Kotra Ureguei from the Union of Workers' Unions and Exploited Kanaks, Gilles Sainati, general secretary of the French magistrates' union and of course François Dufour for the Confédération.

On 13 September 2000 the French courts in Millau finally passed judgment on José Bové and his nine co-accused Three months in prison for Bové himself, two months suspended for Jean-Emile Sanchez, Léon Maillé and Frédéric Libot and between 2,000 and 3,000 franc fines for the rest. Bové, as before refused any compromise and was eventually to serve the remainder of his sentence, after appeals had been exhausted (and the 2002 Presidential campaign was out of the way!) in June–July 2002.

Defence of farmers producing sheep's milk that was unfairly discriminated against by the American embargo on Roquefort, a radical critique of junk food (to which José Bové has applied the evocative French word *malbouffe*), contestation of the globalisation promoted by the WTO: all these themes were united that day, making the dismantling of a few sheets of metal roofing and some electricity fittings the starting point for a real shockwave that reverberated around the entire world.

This was a surprise to those who had not yet noticed the non-corporate character of the Confédération's actions, in other words, the fact that it did not stand for a narrow defence of farmers' corporate interests against those of the wider society. Yes, the eruption of the Confédération onto the scene as one of the most active participants in the social movement was only a surprise for those who had forgotten the mobilisation against the use of hormones in imported American beef, the creation of the Farmers–Ecologists–Consumers Alliance in 1991, which brought together many national organisations, the fight for the prohibition of anabolic steroids in 1996, protests against the patenting of life and against genetically modified organisms from 1997 onwards, the wave of court appearances and mobilisations, occupation of the headquarters of the General Association of Wheat Producers (AGPB) in 1997 to denounce the scandalous division of public monies in agriculture, recourse to the law against illicit practices of all kinds (whether involving hormones, feedstuffs made from animal carcasses – *farines animals* – fraud involving the quality of milk...), mobilisation against agricultural pollution (especially in Brittany), and the permanent world tour undertaken to denounce the disasters of liberal globalisation at Seattle, Bangalore, Nice, Porto Alegre, Davos, Quebec, Genoa, Ouagadougou...

Yes, for those who had forgotten all these interventions

the emergence of the Confédération Paysanne was a surprise. But for the others, even if the extent of the movement transcended all their expectations, it was the legitimate crowning of many decades of resolute, collective work.

Let the struggle continue: at stake is a new CAP, a solidaristic citizens' and farmers' Common Agricultural Policy.

Box 3.2: A trade union struggle with a European dimension

In the early 1980s, when agricultural productivism showed itself for what it was and came into its own, oppositional voices in Europe were scattered. Some informal meetings between the minority trade unions in Germany (ABL), Austria (ÖBV), France (CNSTP), the Netherlands (WBZ) and Switzerland (VKMB) were to lay the foundations for what in 1985 would become the Coordination Paysanne Européene or CPE (the European Farmers Coordination). The CPE organised a meeting in Madrid in December 1986 with 27 participating organisations from eleven different countries on the theme: 'European farmers: competitors or partners?' Since 1987 the CPE has been regularly consulted by the Agricultural Commission of the European Parliament and by the European Commissioner for Agriculture. Some spectacular actions contributed to its recognition: ploughing up the Parliament lawns to protest at the set-aside policy; a Flemish cow to welcome officials at the Commission HQ to draw their attention to the risks of hormones in milk (BST); a farmers' march which helped to bring down a project for a giant henhouse in the Marne which would have housed 5 million laying hens and could have been capable, on its own, of supplying one-tenth of all French egg production.

Without hiding the difficulties of trade unionism at the European level, mainly those of travel and costs of translation, this work is essential to create an alternative to that of the mainstream majority unions (COPA COGECA) whose alliances with the agri-food and agro-industrial firms have made them complicit in the development and application of destructive agricultural policies. The monopoly of representation of these large farmers at the heart of the consultative committee structure of the European Commission lasted until 1999 when the CPE was finally, if only partially, recognised.

The major ambition of the CPE is to have a decisive impact when major policy reviews take place – on the reform of the market regimes and of the CAP itself.

... and an international one, with Via Campesina

Because the EU is subject to the constraints of the free-market agreements, and the CAP accepts an alignment with the WTO Marrakech Agreements, the CPE has worked to develop international relations and to build an alternative to this market globalisation. Via Campesina is an international movement made up of small and medium-sized farmers, agricultural workers, women and peasants as well as rural communities in Asia, Africa, America and Europe. It is an autonomous, pluralist organisation, independent of any political, economic or other movement. It organises in seven regions: Europe, North-West Asia, South-East Asia, North America, the Caribbean, Central America and South America. It also undertakes joint work with African farmers' organisations.

The creation of Via Campesina goes back to 1992 at a meeting in Managua. In 1993 the first Via Campesina international conference was held at Mons in Belgium. It established the movement as a world organisation, defined its constitution and developed its first strategic orientations. Its second conference was at Tiaxcala in Mexico in 1996, where 70 organisations from 37 countries participated. Questions of agrarian reform, debt, development, technology and food sovereignty (see Chapter 4) were discussed. Then it was

Bangalore in India that hosted the third conference. There Via Campesina condemned unequivocally the integration of agriculture and food into the WTO Accords and demanded that they should be taken out of the negotiations. It wants the concept of food sovereignty to be recognised in international law. This claim for food sovereignty, accepted as legitimate in certain international bodies, notably the FAO, affirms the right of peoples to decide their level of food security both quantitatively and qualitatively. It also affirms the right of countries or groups of countries to control imports at their frontiers when the circulation of surplus agricultural produce has destructive effects on producers and on local markets. In its view, dumping by the rich countries serves to reduce the level of self-sufficiency of the poor ones and to enlarge the gap between them and the rich.

Finally, Via Campesina calls for a world audit to evaluate the serious consequences of the introduction of genetically modified organisms (GMOs) into agriculture and emphasises that the constraining policies of structural adjustment imposed by the IMF and the World Bank amplify the mechanisms which impoverish populations and rural milieus. Via Campesina wants to respond to the globalisation of markets and the ever-increasing powers of the transnationals with the globalisation of the trade-union struggle and the addoption of the slogan: 'Let us globalise hope'. Let us envisage another globalisation, that of peoples, of a plurality of cultures and of fair trade.

4 Major principles for changing international policies

We have seen that the Common Agricultural Policy is inextricably linked to the policies of the World Trade Organisation. To modify the former, the European Union would also have to change its stance in international negotiations.

An overview of the 'givens'

The declaration signed at Doha in November 2001 does not bring much change to the world of agriculture. The negotiations confirmed the total lack of credibility of the EU, absurdly committed to its policy of export restitutions, to the point of isolating itself and putting itself in opposition to those it wanted to attract with its 'Everything but Arms' initiative, namely the poor countries. In the end, the agricultural section of the final declaration merely clarified the schedule for renegotiating the original 1994 Agreement on Agriculture. From then on, until the end of March 2003, the parties concerned were committed to reach agreement on the status given to direct payments in the blue box, on the ways of reducing then eliminating export restitutions in the red box and on the level of customs duties and internal supports linked to production in the amber box (see the discussion on the 'boxes' in Chapter 2, pp. 34–36).

The check to the launching of a new round of negotiations at Seattle did not prevent agricultural negotiations continuing within the framework of the WTO Committee on Agriculture. The aims of the negotiators remained, as ever, to limit protectionism by easing access to markets for foreign goods, to suppress the different forms of dumping by harmonising the conditions of export competition and to reduce state support to farmers.

The resulting proliferation of international exchanges would significantly increase the profits of the transnationals specialising in all the links of the chain (merchants, transporters, bankers, insurers etc.) as Via Campesina and ROPPA[1] affirmed in a communiqué of 17 May 2001 when coming out against the 'Everything but Arms' initiative:

> The priority for peasants and their families in the less developed countries (LDCs) is first of all to produce for their families, then to have access to the internal market, long before exporting. The European decision can, on the contrary, only reinforce the profits of the large firms using the resources and the labour power of the LDCs to grow export crops destined for the EU. This will reduce the resources and labour power devoted to the production of food for farming and urban families in each country, thus increasing food insecurity.[2]

Hence the urgent need to change the international 'givens'.

Reaffirm food sovereignty

In absolute terms, the planet produces enough to feed all its inhabitants, even if human pressure is becoming problematic in a number of respects. FAO reports show that agricultural output has grown faster than population over the last 30 years. Famine in the world to date has not been the result of a structural incapacity to produce enough foodstuffs, but rather of a scandalous division of wealth across the world, of armed conflicts, iniquitous land and social policies and predatory commercial policies. Large agricultural exporting countries like Brazil and Argentina (which produce millions of tonnes of soya to fatten European beef and pigs) count a significant part of their populations as not having enough to eat. India, with 200 million malnourished, is a net cereal exporter!

Unlike many other commodities, food is a necessity for everyone. That is why the human right to assured food sovereignty and food security is a fundamental one that must be universally recognised in all international commercial agreements with a bearing on agriculture. And, to guarantee this sovereignty, protection against imports is indispensable, for both North and South. In every country priority must be given to the production of basic foodstuffs while preserving social and environmental conditions. This implies that each country should be in a position to implement agricultural policies compatible with its internal needs. And that includes the right to protect itself against imports, while at the same time putting in place agrarian reforms which will guarantee that farmers have access to land.

This right to protect one's own agriculture becomes even more important as the tendency for food preferences to become homogenised accelerates with globalisation. To export the industrialised countries' hyperconsumption-of-animal-proteins model to the South (the main agent of which is the worldwide diffusion of 'fast food') threatens the long-run ability of these countries to feed populations that are rising rapidly. To produce a kilo of animal protein you need in effect seven kilos of vegetable protein.

The rich countries bear an enormous responsibility for this situation. The food deficit of the Less Developed Countries increased by 60 per cent between 1994 and 1998 (that is, after the signature of the Agreement on Agriculture), and has continued to rise. The contributions of EU Trade Commissioner Pascal Lamy and his associates become even more irresponsible in terms of the supposed advantages to LDCs of liberalising trade and exporting food products:

> The EU is already the largest agricultural importer in the world, much of it from developing countries. In 1997–99, the EU imported more agricultural products from developing countries than the USA, Canada, Japan, Australia and New Zealand combined. This is a good thing.[3]

The effects of the increasing decline in food self-sufficiency inside the LDCs is nowhere referred to.

That is why the Confédération Paysanne, in concert with Via Campesina, has underlined the necessity of a moratorium in WTO negotiations; the annulment of the obligation to allow a minimum of 5 per cent of internal consumption of member states by way of imports (4 per cent in the case of developing countries), and of every clause making market access obligatory. They call instead for a formal recognition of the right of people to protect their agriculture.

Make dumping illegal

If world trade in agricultural products is destructive, it is particularly so because the prices it imposes bear no relation either to the costs of production or to the remuneration of the work of the farmer. It is no longer a question of the honest calculation of comparative advantages, as neoliberal economic theory would have it, but of commercially dishonest practices, because the most powerful actors benefit from public aid and the weakest do not. Remember that the aid to productivist agriculture in France had risen by the turn of the millennium to €11 billion for 650,000 farming units, that is almost €17,000 on average, the equivalent of the average farm income – and this excludes social security payments! The progressive elimination of export restitutions that do not conform to the WTO agreements, and their dressing up in the guise of multifunctionality in the green box simply reproduces, in new form, the same disconnection between agricultural prices and costs of production.

From its side, the politics of the USA, instituted by its FAIR Act of 1996, by suppressing anything that existed by way of constraints on production, has brought structural overproduction in its wake. The US Congress has had to multiply the number of emergency budgetary bailouts in order to save farmers in distress, so much so that they became annual affairs before the new Farm Security and Rural Investment Act of 2002 raised the levels of subsidy to a staggering $18 billion a year (see Box 5.1).

We must oppose economic dumping, just as we must social and environmental dumping (that is the movement of production to areas where social and environmental controls are minimal or ineffective). A policy of import controls, the only policy available to poor countries, linked to plans of action to create the conditions which will allow a return to prices that reward farmers adequately for their work, will allow a certain integrity to return to the markets.

Thus the Confédération Paysanne calls for multilateral and bilateral agreements which recognise reciprocal rights to food sovereignty rather than to 'free trade'.

The desire to accelerate the liberalisation of markets regardless of cost, despite the setbacks encountered at the multilateral level at the end of the 1990s (notably with the defeats of the MAI – the Multilateral Agreement on Investment – in December 1998 and at Seattle a year later) led the EU to multiply bilateral agreements or projects for free trade, in particular with the majority of countries of the

South, in Africa and Latin America since 1995. In doing so, it was following in the wake of the USA and Canada which together with Mexico had formed NAFTA (the North American Free Trade Agreement) in 1994, an association they are now transforming into the Free Trade Zone of the Americas from 2005.

In addition to the EU agreements with eleven Mediterranean countries, South Africa and Mexico, and the scheduling of agreements for economic partnership between the EU and 77 ACP countries from 2008 (the Cotonou Agreement, May 2000), negotiations are chugging along with Mercosur (the South American Cone common market: Argentina, Brazil, Paraguay and Uruguay, with which Chile is associated).[4]

The Mercosur countries are attempting to play off the USA and the EU against one another in order to get the largest possible opening up of Western markets to their agricultural and food exports. At the same time, they have denounced the export subsidies of both as undermining a level playing field.

Despite the talk of putting a desire to develop the poor counties to the forefront, thanks to an extended partnership, these free-trade agreements have characteristics in common. First, each of these agreements is made with reference to and alongside the WTO rules, which are based on deregulation and elimination of any barriers to trade, particularly customs barriers. Second, they have been concluded between countries at very different levels of economic development. As Gérard Surdez of ATTAC Marseille put it:

> Although they are all today theoretically independent, the current situation is not without echoes of the nineteenth century when the great colonial empires of Europe, on the one hand, and the United States (based on the Monroe doctrine) on the other,

controlled the countries of the South, in theory to 'civilise' them, but in reality to use them to develop their merchant navies and their industries.[5]

The large majority of these agreements undertake to reduce the debt of the countries of the South and to contribute to financing their economic and social development, while imposing on them, in the grand tradition of the IMF, drastic reductions in public expenditure, involving the dismantling and the privatisation of their public sectors for the greater profit of the transnationals of the North.

Reality is thus the obverse of the enticing neoliberal rhetoric. These agreements will have dramatic consequences for farmers, in the South as in the North. According to Karen Lehman of the Mexican National Union of Autonomous Regional Peasant organisations, a network of half a million small-scale grain, coffee, livestock and wood product producers: 'In NAFTA, Mexico sacrificed protection for the peasant farming sector, and for food security itself, in exchange for increased exports of fruit and vegetables.'[6] More broadly, 'the experience of Mexico since NAFTA shows that commercial opening-up to a country with a much higher level of development provokes a deindustrialisation, the liquidation of entire swathes of traditional agriculture and a growth in social inequality.'[7] All of this has led Mexican peasant organisations to join the Via Campesina in order to demand that trade in agricultural produce be removed from the competence of the WTO.

Box 4.1: Mexico: a case study

Mexico joined the GATT in 1986 and the North American Free Trade Agreement (NAFTA) soon after. This agreement, between Mexico, the United States and Canada, came into effect on 1 January 1994. All sorts of benefits were envisaged as liberal models predicted such things as:

- A fall in Mexican maize output as domestic prices fell in the NAFTA area.
- The release of labour, land and capital for more 'productive' activities; in agriculture this would involve diversification into other crops and particularly labour-intensive horticultural ones.
- Ensuing environmental benefits as marginal lands, vulnerable to erosion, were left fallow.

How has it all turned out? Oxfam GB and WWF International commissioned Dr Alejandro Nadal to carry out a study of the effects of Mexico's liberalisation on its agricultural sector. Published in September 2000 it came to what the sponsors called a conclusion 'both simple and stark: liberalization has failed to achieve the environmental and social improvements it promised.'[8]

Maize was first cultivated in Mexico 5,000 years ago. Its cultivation has been entwined with the social and economic fabric of the population for millennia. Nowhere is maize more genetically diverse than it is in Mexico, with 41 racial complexes and thousands of maize varieties recognized there. It is the most important single crop in the economy with 8 per cent of the population (40 per cent of those working in agriculture) directly dependent on it. Some 60 per cent of the land under cultivation is devoted to it.

But for NAFTA it was 'inefficient'. The US Corn Belt produces 8 tonnes of maize per hectare, compared with Mexico's 1.8. But no account was made of the social and environmental costs of US methods of production, nor of the social and environmental benefits of the Mexican system, which is heavily reliant on locally adapted varieties of which its farmers were the unpaid guardians.

Nor was there any in-depth analysis of the possible effects of the liberalisation process. As Nadal says, in a model of understatement, the decision to liberalise markets 'was based more on ideology than careful analysis of the facts'. At best, there was some recognition of the shock that free trade would cause, so a 15-year transition period was agreed. Yet in practice this was 'compressed' by a gung-ho liberal government to around 18 months! From January to August 1996 the home price of maize fell by 48 per cent, converging with the world price 12 years earlier than envisaged. At the same time, the Mexican state drastically reduced its support for agriculture.

The results were predictable and the situation that has developed with liberalisation and associated government policies is a litany of disaster. The situation of rural farmers, especially maize producers, has become increasingly desperate.

- Maize prices dropped sharply but did not result in lower consumer prices for maize products. Indeed, tortilla (maize flat-bread) prices actually rose.
- Many less profitable farmers have been forced to cultivate even less productive lands or gone out of business altogether and flocked to the towns where they join the ranks of the unemployed, or, if possible, to the USA as illegal migrants
- Women have generally been the ones left behind to try to look after the children. With little money they have to seek whatever rural employment they can find; and the children's education is often abruptly interrupted, as they are withdrawn from school to work in the fields.[9]
- At the same time the output of Mexican maize has not fallen – surprisingly it has remained remarkably stable as new, ever more marginal, land has been pressed into use by small farmers trying to eke out a living while getting lower returns for any maize they are able to sell.

- Overall consumption has increased, but largely due to the use of cheap maize as cattle feed or in industry.
- The agricultural diversification that was predicted did not occur. As maize prices dropped so did those of possible substitute crops, and maize remained relatively more profitable. Nor were labour-intensive horticultural crops able to absorb the labour and land released from maize production.
- Migration and the weakening of social institutions are contributing to genetic erosion, as traditional knowledge of maize seeds is lost and Mexico's amazing genetic diversity threatened.
- Mexico prohibits the growing of genetically modified maize, but still allows it to be imported (about a fifth of US maize is now genetically modified). Evidence is accumulating of it finding its way into native crops.
- Soil erosion is accelerating with the trend to specialisation and monoculture; and the use of marginal land as mentioned above.
- Maize requires intensive irrigation and water is being extracted from many Mexican aquifers faster than they are being replenished; in addition, salinisation and accumulation of chemical residues are widespread.
- Pollution from agriculture has increased dramatically with the use of heavy nitrogenous fertilizer in the commercial sector.
- Pollution is not confined to Mexico. As maize production in the USA intensifies, especially in the dry climate areas of cultivation that require heavy irrigation, the same pollution effects are visible: aquifer draining, fertiliser run-offs, and rapidly increasing pesticide use as the corn borer flourishes.[10]

But maybe the benefits have been felt by US and Canadian farmers? Not so. In June 2001 *Public Citizen* published a report called 'Down on the Farm: Seven-Years War on Farmers and Ranchers in the US, Canada and Mexico' on the effects of seven years of NAFTA on the farmers in all three countries involved.[11] Its conclusion is stark, summed up in the sub-title of the report: 'Dwindling incomes for small farmers in the US, Mexico and Canada, lost farms and rural crisis is NAFTA's legacy.'

The *New York Times* is not noted for its radicalism but its editorial on 1 December 2002 headed 'The Hypocrisy of Farm Subsidies' pulled no punches:

> When Mexican corn farmers tramp through their fields behind donkey-drawn plows, they have one goal: to eke out a living. Increasingly, however, they find themselves saddled with mountains of unsold produce because farmers in Kansas and Nebraska sell their own corn in Mexico at prices well below those of the Mexicans. This is not primarily due to higher efficiency. The Americans' real advantage comes from huge taxpayer-provided subsidies that allow them to sell overseas at 20 percent below the actual cost of production. In other words, we subsidize our farmers so heavily that they can undersell poor competitors abroad. And just to make sure, we have tariff barriers in place that make it extremely hard for many third world farmers to sell in the United States. The same is true for their efforts to sell in Europe and Japan. The world's farming system is in favor of the rich.

The bilateral agreements already concluded or still being negotiated by the EU with countries of the South, which for the most part are less industrialised than Mexico, will have even more dramatic consequences for their farmers and the majority of poor people, since the factors of production (land, water resources, irrigation infrastructure etc.) diverted to support export produce cannot but raise the prices of subsistence goods and impede the development of their basic foodstuffs. In Brazil, for instance, 'neoliberal economic policy, stimulating agribusiness imports in return for national agribusiness exports of the large Brazilian enterprises, is severely damaging to small and medium-sized farmers, who suffer from social exclusion and the loss of their lands'.[12] While certain family farmers producing soya gain from the heavy European imports benefit, 'these also contribute to the destruction of the jobs of their colleagues, both in Europe and in all countries affected by the dumping of the EU's animal production'. The International Fund for Agricultural Development (IFAD) has recently revealed that:

> Almost 64 per cent of the rural population in Latin America and the Caribbean live below the poverty line and, over the last two decades, the number of poor people in rural areas has increased in both absolute and relative terms.[13]

And this in a region where the 'poorest 20 per cent of the population receive only 3 per cent of all income; the wealthiest 20 per cent receive 60 per cent'.[14] The risks are even greater for black Africa's farmers, whose productivity is but one-thousandth that of their European 'equivalents'. The FAO in a 1999 symposium on the effects of the AoA stressed with regard to Senegal that :

> Liberalisation measures undertaken since the 1980s and the 50 per cent devaluation of the CFA franc in 1994 have not improved the competitive position of the agricultural sector which has been facing difficulties due to import competition (e.g. dairy products, rice, onions and sugar).[15]

In this context it is necessary to condemn the signing of such free-trade agreements and to demand, as with the WTO, a moratorium on all negotiations and agreements extending the scope and the diffusion of free trade to agricultural and food products. The rich countries, in particular the EU, must modify their policies of cooperation. The priority must be the promotion of macro-regional groupings which integrate developing countries with similar structures and comparable produce and with protection of their internal agricultural markets.

What holds for the countries of the South is equally valid for the countries of central and eastern Europe. Their entry into the core of the EU must be preceded by a transitional phase during which, with financial support from the EU, these countries give priority to the establishment of a long-term employment-oriented agriculture that is ecologically, economically and socially durable.

In general, the agreements concluded between the EU and the countries of the South, as with the WTO agreements, must be subordinate to the 1948 Universal Declaration of Human Rights, the International Covenant on Economic, Social and Cultural Rights, ratified in 1966 by the General Assembly of the United Nations (whose article 11 recognises 'the fundamental right of everyone to be free from hunger') and to international conventions relating to social rights and to the environment.

5 Fateful choice for the CAP

Since July 2002, the European agricultural landscape has been in turmoil. Even if the Berlin Accords of 1999 included provision for many meetings spread over 2002 to 2003, nobody really expected the Commission to propose a new – and profound – change in the rules of the game, barely three years after the previous reform. Yet that is precisely what it did.

Many factors pushed it in this direction.

First was the enlargement of the EU envisaged for 2004. This will irrevocably overturn the precarious equilibrium of European agriculture. The 30 per cent increase in the number of farmers who are potential beneficiaries of the CAP and the increase in the diversity of 'models' of agriculture in the Union makes the maintenance of the status quo improbable, indeed dangerous – especially as the cost of such enlargement reinforces the concern of those countries, Germany to the fore, that wish to reduce their contribution to the agricultural budget.

Another tangible reason is the renewal of the agricultural negotiations within the WTO since March 2003 in Geneva. The mandate from Doha two years earlier imposes the obligation on all participants to reach agreement before 2005 on such matters as the status of direct aids in the blue box, the modalities of reduction and then elimination of export restitutions (the red box), and the level of reduction of custom duties and internal subsidies linked to production (the amber box).

Parallel to this, the Cairns Group denunciations of the dumping practices of the EU have become more and more strident. Brazil, for instance, has forced the convening of a WTO panel to seek the suppression of EU support for beet sugar, a hearing the EU might well lose.

A false opposition

In this context there is a confrontation between two apparently conflicting logics in the debates which have shaken the Europe of the 15 since the Berlin Accords.

The strategy of the status quo

This logic aims to preserve agriculture as it is: intensive, export-oriented – and protected. It is the good old precept: 'free to win and protected from losing'. This strategy is defended by groups which have traditionally been the beneficiaries of the CAP: the agri-food industry, cooperative and private suppliers, food processors, merchants and agri-managers who above all profit from public subsidies and the restructuring of agriculture. This agro-industrial complex is well organised in the large networks of production. Neo-liberal agricultural trade unionism, represented in Europe by COPA-COGECA[1] (which includes the FNSEA in the case of France and the National Farmers Unions of England and Wales, Scotland and Ulster for the United Kingdom) is the most vociferous expression of this interest group, one which was well-satisfied by the conclusions of Agenda 2000, despite its public protestations against it. Not surprisingly, as its members profited from it! COPA-COGECA is quite prepared to negotiate new price reductions in return for compensation through increases in subsidies.

Recourse to techniques of production such as GMOs, growth hormones and feedstuffs containing animal protein have been demanded in terms of the 'right to be modern': the right, that is, of Community processing industries to acquire their basic inputs at the lowest possible price and thus to consolidate their competitiveness in world markets! This approach accepts the cohabitation of a dual agriculture which assures the co-existence of, on the one hand, a large-scale agriculture that is 'competitive and open on the international markets' but subsidised, and on the other hand, a commercial niche agriculture, strongly linked to regions (e.g. Burgundian wines, Parma hams, *pré salé* lamb from the saltmarshes of Brittany and Normandy, and the like), respecting the environment and more oriented towards marks of quality.

To win society's support and thus to make the ever-increasing budgetary costs of such a scenario acceptable, its defenders say they are ready to make environmental efforts (particularly through industry-promoted schemes such as 'agriculture raisonnée' in France, or 'Little Red Tractor' or 'Farm Assured' labels in Britain).[2] These are at best forms of large-scale industrial agriculture modified on the edges and do little if anything to protect the environment, animal welfare or food quality.

By refusing to change their model of agriculture, despite the intense frenzy of the last three years, these defenders of the logic of the status quo are preparing a first-class funeral for the farming world.

Green liberalism, the other false solution

In response to the preceding scenario, defended by the agri-food industry, a new and unexpected alliance has emerged. It centres on those pushing for the dismantling of national and regional institutions such as the CAP whenever they impede their freedom of movement, with the transnational firms as its spearhead. The aim is to accelerate the restructuring of

European agriculture by anticipating the delocalisation of production. Why continue to support the 'competitiveness' of European agriculture to obtain low-cost inputs if you can obtain the same commodities on the world market at half the price without subsidy?

This current, praising to the skies the all-powerful nature of the market in whichever domain of the economy, wants to proscribe any public intervention in the regulation of agricultural exchanges. But what makes for the originality of this discourse – and its danger – is its opening towards environmentalism in its recognition that, in the rich countries, agriculture produces a certain number of services in the collective interest (positive amenities such as environmental protection, maintenance of space, occupation of land) which constitute public goods to which society is attached but which the market does not know how to reward.

The state, which this lobby condemns in other respects, is here called on to reward these non-remunerative services by making agricultural subsidies conditional on respect for certain environmental criteria. This is the now famous 'decoupling' of subsidies: subsidies which are not linked directly either to production or to agricultural prices.

This new magic word 'decoupling' has enabled a de facto alliance – one that might be thought unnatural – between neoliberals and certain representatives of ecological politics. The latter have come to believe, naively (often because they have no understanding of the reality and the role of agricultural policies in the regulation of markets), that a partially ecological agriculture – one that combines low prices and high subsidies decoupled from production and subject to certain environmental criteria – is possible. The highly organised animal welfare lobby is to be found among these actors. Deeply rooted in the UK, it has seen its legitimate concerns taken up – and corrupted – by those whose sole concern is to see the CAP abolished.

The latter explain fervently that because the CAP has led to the disaster that we all recognise, it is intrinsically bad to support agriculture in any form. They imply that to suppress it altogether would be a lesser evil! These arguments suggest that a progressive dismantling of the CAP coupled with specific measures in favour of improved methods of animal rearing will allow a substantial improvement in the methods of production. The ecology movements of the countries traditionally attached to free trade have allowed themselves to be taken in and have come gradually to believe in them. How can they not see that falling agricultural prices will induce a race to the bottom, a drive to secure the lowest costs of production and thus will favour the continued industrialisation of production, in Europe if environmental regulation permits, otherwise elsewhere?

Furthermore, these new 'allies' claim that the replacement of the current support system by decoupled subsidies will eliminate any distortion of trade, something economists of stature denounce as an enormous deception as shown in Chapter 1 above.

This pressure group presents a particular danger in that, by buying into the positions of the environmental movement, it has allowed the link between those struggling against the CAP and those struggling against uncontrolled globalisation of agricultural exchanges to be broken. It is the expression of a compromise that is willing to exchange a residual, clean European agriculture (made inviting by a new type of farmer: the farmer as 'gardener of rural space') against the total freedom of action of agri-food producers on the European markets. Rather than subsidising the production of cereals to produce pork in polluting European battery farms, is it not preferable to preserve the environment at home and to buy pork from poor countries with low wages and with less constraining environmental legislation? This prospect is no longer fiction – it is the strategy already adopted by the firm

Doux, which has built its supremacy in poultry worldwide by delocalising part of its processing to South America, closer to its protein suppliers (see Box 1.3). An important French sugar refinery is following suit in case the sugar regime is dismantled

Towards a reform of the CAP in 2003

The Commission clearly leans towards the second of these two scenarios. Its principal preoccupation today is to find the necessary support within society for the deregulation of agricultural markets. This was clearly expressed in the EC's Comprehensive Negotiating Proposal for the WTO, adopted by the Agricultural Committee at its extraordinary session on 20–21 November 2000:

> The EC believe that further liberalisation and expansion of trade for agricultural products are an important contribution to sustained and continued economic growth, in both developed and developing countries. The EC believe that in order to achieve these goals, it is vital to muster strong public support, which can only be achieved if other concerns are met, in particular the multifunctional role of agriculture, which covers the protection of the environment and the sustained vitality of rural communities, food safety and other consumer concerns including animal welfare.[3]

Making this strategy into official policy, the European Commission announced its proposals for mid-term reform of the CAP in July 2002. The package was really attractively wrapped, the words carefully chosen to keep the citizens on-side, with the press release headed: 'Farm policy cannot turn a blind eye to society's expectations'.

So Commissioner Franz Fischler announced in his

presentation that changes were needed to restore the CAP's credibility:

> We need a fresh start for the sake of the farmer, the consumer and the taxpayer. If we are serious about a policy which promotes quality rather than quantity, which offers farmers incentives not to produce for intervention stocks and not to gear their production to subsidy levels but to what the consumer wants, which frees farmers from the bureaucratic yoke of form-filling and which improves the standing of our farm aid schemes with the general public in the EU and with the WTO, then we have to decouple direct payments from production and make them conditional on compliance with environment, food safety and animal welfare standards.[4]

Such talk had enough in it to convince credulous spirits or those ignorant of the realities. What had to happen happened. The media threw themsleves onto the statement and Fischler's proposals were presented as the reforms consumers had been hankering after for years, an ambitious reform that would bring the productivist lobby to heel. There was no shortage of superlatives to describe the revolution that was supposed to have taken place.

Reality was less attractive. By the merest chance, the Commission had failed to spell out the full significance of its reform proposals in relation to control of markets and opening up of frontiers.

Looked at more closely, the project bears little resemblance to Franz Fischler's fine words. There really was a passing off of shoddy goods.

The Commission's project is more an attempt to emulate the US FAIR Act of 1996 than anything else. This is particularly ironic in that , six years after its introduction, Congress decided to abandon this policy because of its disastrous consequences for US farmers (including a complete disruption of markets, fall in agricultural exchange rates, and an explosion of the emergency aid budget – see Box 5.1).

To make this complex debate intelligible, let us rapidly decode the Commission's proposals. Why should the reforms proposed by Fischler favour in reality neither an agriculture of quality nor respect for the environment?

Contrary to appearances, this project has no goal other than to adapt the CAP to the recommendations of the WTO. It is a matter, first and foremost, of making direct subsidies WTO-compliant by the mechanism of decoupling the entirety of production subsidies. The inclusive subsidy given to farm establishments in the Fischler plan, in addition to freezing the current distribution of subsidies and thus the current injustices, paves the way for the end of any policy of market management, already badly disrupted by the reforms of 1992 and 1999. The Commission's proposals would allow the beneficiaries of decoupled subsidies to produce without restraints (other than those of a phoney ecology), to produce what they want and eventually to change their production each year. So it would be goodbye to any control of outputs, and welcome to market and agricultural price instability.

On the other hand, many measures aim to reinforce the competitiveness of the EU on world agricultural markets, thanks particularly to a new reduction in the intervention price for cereals which would have the effect of bringing their price closer to world market levels.

Finally, the Commission's desire is to make Europe ever more accessible to imports from third countries. What blindness, to encourage the production of more, and less expensively, of what we already produce at low cost and in surplus, and to increase the imports of those crops – oil seeds and vegetable proteins – in which the EU is most deficient (to the tune of 70 per cent) and which, if produced at home, would allow European producers to establish a semblance of self-sufficiency. To feed battery poultry, they would rather we import transgenic soya than replace some millions of hectares of wheat with leguminous plants

As soon as the proposals had been enunciated, reactions flooded in and a diplomatic ballet could begin. There was nothing surprising about it – nor anything reassuring. With a banging of fists on the table, the French, Spanish and Irish governments defended the strategy of the status quo. The Berlin Accords of 1999 envisaged a renegotiation in 2006; nothing justified a reform of any kind now! On the other side, the UK, Sweden and the Netherlands demanded that the Commission go faster, further! Sitting in the middle, Germany repeated to whoever would listen that the Fischler project perhaps wasn't bad, but that the Commission had not responded to the demands for a reduction in the net budgetary contribution which Germany made to the CAP.

This strictly financial approach was nothing new, but here it took on an importance it had never had before. Each country was trying to limit its contribution, to ensure it had a net positive return: that is, that its receipts from the Community's agricultural budget exceeded its contributions to it. This narrow budgetary logic prevented any truly fundamental discussion. For all that, if the Confédération Paysanne has affirmed the need to agree the policy objectives for agriculture before any discussion on the budget and to demystify the rule of 'rate of return' considerations, it cannot deny that the stakes in this debate concern the future of the Union. For a long time, Europe, and notably agricultural Europe, was built on the Franco-German alliance, at the heart of which France has largely imposed its views thanks to being the world's fourth-ranked economic power, and above all Europe's foremost agricultural power. Profiting from this domination, France had until now largely been successful in imposing its financial policy orientations and budgetary interests. From a financial point of view, France has been the country that was able to profit most from this manna from Europe, gaining for its agriculture a greater return from the European budget than it contributed.

This situation began to change both politically and economically after the fall of the Berlin Wall in 1989 and the rapid integration of East Germany into the Federal Republic, making Germany today the giant of Europe whether from a demographic, an economic or a political perspective. If, in the framework of Agenda 2000, France managed to wrest a still largely favourable budgetary return (23.6 per cent pay back from the agricultural budget for a contribution of 16 per cent) it was at a price of intensive bargaining which has left its traces.

These sometimes robust debates on the budget were intertwined with another, equally important to the future of the Union. On 9 October 2002 the European Commission recommended that the negotiations on accession to the European Union should be concluded by the end of the year with Cyprus, the Czech Republic, Estonia, Hungary, Latvia, Lithuania, Malta, Poland, the Slovak Republic and Slovenia, for entry on 1 May 2004. But no agreement had yet been reached as to the conditions under which some (over 4 million!) farmers in these countries were to be disposed of.

Germany's fear, but also that of Sweden and the Netherlands and in a less clearly articulated way that of a majority of the Europe of the 15, was once again strictly budgetary. To distribute to the farmers of the eight new countries the same levels of subsidy as the current beneficiaries in the 15 were receiving spelled certain financial disaster. Germany therefore chose the strong-arm method of making its 'partners' see reason. So strong indeed that it risked compromising the principle of enlargement and sowing mayhem at the heart of the EU. Its position was: 'We're in favour of the entry of the CEECs but without direct support for their farmers' – a winning strategy for Germany but a losing one for European farmers, those of the CEECs included.

Finally, on the eve of the European Council meeting of heads of member states which was to adopt the modalities – particularly financial – and the definitive timetable for the integration of the eight new members, the Franco-German alliance was put into motion again and a Franco-German accord signed. The next day, 25 October, at the eleventh hour, the heads of state of the 15 adopted a position whose main point was to put a ceiling on CAP expenditure between 2006 and 2013 at the level to be reached in 2006. During this same period the subsidies paid to the new member states would rise progressively to that of their colleagues in the old Europe.

A real revolution

What is the significance of this last-minute agreement?

This decision comes down to the enlarged EU spending the same amount on 23 member states (and 11.5 million farmers) as it currently spends on the 7 million farmers of the EU-15.

Contrary to what is commonly claimed, agricultural policy does not ruin European taxpayers. The budget devoted to farmers, who represent 3 to 4 per cent of the economically active European population, is no more than 0.5 per cent of the GDP of the EU. And if this money – currently very unjustly distributed – represents around 40 per cent of the Community budget, this reveals above all the restricted size of the total budget and with it the crippling poverty of social policy within the EU, and member states' unwillingness to project and support any wider vision of it.

[87]

For the Confédération Paysanne it is not a question of making Europe into a milch cow for agriculture. What costs so much today is not the agricultural budget as such, but the consequential costs of the disastrous policy choices of an intensive, industrial agriculture with its environmental spillovers, a deregulation of markets with its social consequences, the costs associated with BSE and so on.

That is why the decision to put a ceiling on agricultural expenditure, unless followed by radical changes in the orientation of the CAP, will have fateful consequences for the farmers of the Europe of the 15 and even more so for those of the countries of central and eastern Europe.

The farmers of the current EU, suffering since 1992 from a generalised fall in agricultural prices, find their income now essentially made up of compensation payments from the EU. If there is not a substantial rise in agricultural prices to accompany the capping of the budget, the direct consequence will be a substantial fall in farmers' income. Simply put, a reduction in the per capita budget translates into a reduction in aid received. The proposals for a 'dynamic modulation of subsidies' formulated by the Commission, has – masked by the talk of redistribution and the financing of rural political interventions – no other objective than to prepare for this drastic fall.

The agricultural world has seen a restructuring without precedent: in the name of competitiveness and the export vocation of European agriculture, 2 million farms have disappeared in ten years in almost total silence. Now the EU is preparing a new bloodletting in the countryside, in reality turning its back on the objective of preserving the multi-functionality of agriculture. It is hard to mention this concept without a wry smile, given that fewer than 2 million farms are scheduled to survive in Europe.

Entry into the EU will have devastating consequences for the farmers in the CEECs, even if the subsidies they receive constitute an undeniable benefit in the short term. A change in agricultural policy seems to us the *sine qua non* of their successful integration into the heart of the Union. If there is no such change, what will entry into the EU represent for the million small farmers who will disappear in Poland alone, if not the promise of economic debacle, the loss of their roots, and exile?

The further decisions of the Council of Agricultural Ministers on 26 June 2003 showed clearly that the EU is determined to drive ahead with a policy that will prove disastrous to farming as a way of life in Europe (see Appendix 4).[5] It is full steam ahead with the implementation of decoupling subsides, even if countries have been given freedom to phase the policy in over a period up to 2007. Hailed as a transformation of how Europe's farmers are supported, it will merely hasten the concentration of farming we have witnessed to date. Farmgate prices will fall and small farms, which get little or no support, will be unable to sustain the slump in their incomes. Judging by experiences to date in Europe, the USA and elsewhere, it will be agribusiness and not the consumers who reap the benefit.

The reality is that the EU wants decoupled subsidies at all costs in order to fit its subsidy system into the green box of the AoA, thus freeing itself of any obligation to reduce them further. This is a choice to continue dumping produce abroad at prices well below their real costs of production rather than adjusting supply to demand within the EU itself. The fact is that developing countries will have their ability to resist dumping and disruption of their agricultures even further reduced by these latest reforms of the CAP.

Yet another policy remains possible, one for a solidaristic Common Agricultural Policy for Europe's citizens and farmers. It is a programme that will be spelled out in the following chapter.

Box 5.1: The new agricultural policy of the United States

With the passing of the 'Farm Security and Rural Investment Act of 2002' in May, the United States government agreed to spend a staggering $18 billion a year on agricultural support over the next ten years. Compare this with the $6 billion that the G8 agreed in July 2002 for NEPAD (New Partnership for African Development) or even the $2 billion set aside for New York relief and reconstruction after September 11. American farmers, it would appear are living the life of Riley.

It's not so simple.

Opposition to the new Farm Act was widespread. Developing countries saw it as heralding a new era of food dumped onto world markets below production cost. American allies in the Cairns Group, that coalition of agricultural exporters which includes Australia, Argentina, Chile, New Zealand and others, were appalled that the USA, spearheading free market reform at the WTO, should compromise its leadership in this way. The EU delivered a blistering attack on the US Act, with Javier Solana, Europe's foreign policy chief, declaring in Madrid in June 2002 that the new American agriculture policy had created the 'most profound' division between Europe and the United States, worse than disputes over steel tariffs, the Kyoto environmental treaty or the International Criminal Court. Country after country has threatened to challenge the USA before the WTO court.

The stinging criticism prompted House Agricultural Committee Chair Larry Combest to remark: 'This bill is not for rural Mexico; it's not for rural Canada; it's not for rural Europe – it's for rural America.' So, we might assume that American small farmers would be cock-a-hoop over the new bill.

Nothing could be further from the truth. American small farmers, just like those in the European Union are facing massive economic pressure and their ability to survive is declining dramatically year after year. 'The 2002 Farm Bill spells disaster for family farmers,' said Bill Christison, a Missouri grain farmer, President of the Missouri Rural Crisis Center and the National Family Farm Coalition. From 1967 to 1992 there was a net loss of 32,500 farms a year. In 1997 the USA had 329,000 fewer farmers than it had a decade earlier. In 1920 there were 925,000 black farmers; by the end of the century there were fewer than 18,000 left. As recently as 1996, according to the US Department of Agriculture, barely half the remaining farmsteads – 985,718 of them – registered a positive net cash return while the rest – 926,108 – showed a net cash loss.

The truth is that US farming is in a state of ongoing crisis – and has been since the 1970s. Farmers are caught in a spiral of rising costs for their inputs and falling prices for the outputs. Between 1987 and 1997 the cost to farmers of seeds, fertiliser and agricultural chemicals alone increased 86 per cent. Thus, while farmers received $123 billion for their animal and crop products, they paid out $185.1 billion in production expenses.

But surely falling farm gate prices must be good for the American consumer? Unfortunately not. Since 1984, the real price of a USDA market basket of food has increased 2.8 per cent while the farm value of that food has fallen by 35.7 per cent. To bring the reality home during the passage of the new Farm Bill, farmers served an $8 meal to legislators and charged only 37c, the value they got for their produce at the farm gate – under 5 per cent of the final value.

So who was the Farm Bill for? As Iowa farmer and Iowa Citizens for Community Improvement member Larry Ginter put it: 'This is a Factory Farm Bill that rips off family farmers and taxpayers, and lines the pockets of the packers and grain traders. Who in America, besides the lobbyists, politicians and agribusiness corporations, actually supports this bill?'

That is the nub. US agriculture, like that in most of the

industrialised world today, is heavily concentrated in the hands of transnationals. In the States, half-a-dozen corporations – Cargill (the world's largest private corporation), Archer Daniels Midland, Tyson Foods, ConAgra and Chiquita International (recently United Brands and before that United Fruit) – totally dominate 'agribusiness', a term which covers everything from financing to producing, manufacturing, transporting, wholesaling and distributing not just the food grown, but also machinery, fertilisers, chemical pesticides, seed, feed and packaging materials.

Most farming subsidies, in the USA as in Europe, end up in the pockets of those who need them least. In 1997 the top 4 per cent of farms, measured by value of sales, took 20 per cent of the new payments introduced by the 1996 Fair (Federal Agricultural Improvement and Reform) Act; another study by the US Environmental Working Group found that 10 per cent of farms received 61 per cent of the payments made under the main forms of direct payment. The American Corn Growers' Association President Keith Dittrich put it simply: 'Rural America is going bankrupt, and this new bill does nothing to reverse this dismal trend.' In the period from 1996 to 1998, the top 1 per cent of subsidy recipients collected an average of $83,000 a year; at the same time fully half of all subsidy recipients were paid less than $1,200 per year.

To understand the new Farm Act of 2002 it is necessary to go back to that previous big reform of 1996. The FAIR Act was dubbed 'Freedom to Farm' by its bipartisan supporters at the time – and 'Freedom to Fail' by US small farmers today!

In the context of the Agreement on Agriculture, the whole basis of agricultural support in the USA was restructured. Those who argued that agriculture was special and could not respond to market signals like any other product lost out to those who believed that taking the government out of agriculture would lead to a self-regulation of supply and demand. Lower prices would lead to an increase in exports; lower prices would also lead to farmers planting fewer acres.

So the new bill ended the 1930s New Deal system of production controls, eliminating federal price supports. Set-aside was suppressed, as was storage of surpluses, whether public (via the 'non-recourse loan rate' whereby farmers were lent money against crops stored as collateral) or private ('farm-owned reserve'). Instead the Act guaranteed a transition period of fixed but declining payments to farmers to end in 2002, when the new market philosophy would have established its inexorable logic.

By 1998 it was already clear that things were not working out as predicted. It led to neither the promised increase in exports nor to the expected price of crops. In the five years to 2000, exports of corn, wheat, soybeans and sorghum dropped by nearly 10 per cent. Prices too cascaded down, with corn falling 41 per cent, wheat 45 per cent and sorghum 50 per cent in the same period, as surpluses that might otherwise have been stored found their way onto the markets.

Massive supplementary payments were introduced as one-offs, then repeated as emergency packages year after year. Total direct payments to US farmers amounted to $12.4 billion in 1998, $21.5 billion in 1999, $22.7 billion in 2000, $20.7 billion in 2001 and $17 billion in 2002.

Bizarrely, these subsidies are acceptable under the AoA because they are either 'decoupled', that is not related directly to what farmers grow nor how much they grow of it, or can be squeezed into the amber box.[6]

These subsidies, it is argued, do not interfere in any substantive way with market mechanisms of price formation. But today, with such high levels of annual subsidy consolidated into a long-term support structure, the idea that $20 billion a year injected into US agriculture has no effect on markets or prices is, frankly, laughable.

In particular, low commodity prices – often well below the direct costs of production – which are the bane of the small farmer, are exactly what commodity traders thrive on.[7] And when concentration of ownership has virtually removed any choice for farmers as to who they sell to, it is not hard to understand how the massive subsidies to farming end up in the pockets of every other sector of agriculture but that of the small farmer.

In most developed western countries (Britain is a notable exception), there is a strong ideological attachment to the idea of the 'farming community' and associated rural values of sturdy self-reliance. It is a notion still assiduously fostered, often by the larger farmers and their organisations who have done so much to undermine it. Agriculture today covers a wide range of often divergent interests: farmers may produce the food, but the profits are made in the farm input, food processing and wholesaling and retailing industries. And even farmers are not all the same: the giant industrialised grain and beef barons, linked directly into the transnational marketing chains, bear little resemblance to even successful small farmers with their modest turnovers and even more modest profit margins.

And yet society for too long has turned a blind eye to agriculture, especially in Britain. The triumph that the repeal of the Corn Laws in 1846 represented against the 'agricultural interest' has come down to us as a 'cheap food' policy, a way of subsidising inadequate wage or benefit levels. So instead of trying to think through exactly what it is we want from our farmers – what kind and quality of food, what sort of countryside – we blame them for all the associated ills of modern farming: polluted food, polluted rivers, cruelty to animals.

The 2002 Farm Act is not a break with this recent past but a consolidation of the trend to take direct government intervention out of agriculture. As Sophia Murphy points out: 'It simply makes US policy a little more transparent.' But, transparent or not, it is the wrong policy – if, that is, you are concerned about the quality of food or the nature of farming or the quality of animal welfare or pesticide use or the run-off of nitrates from fertiliser into the water supply or the effects of agriculture on the countryside generally.

Yet, what is needed is not too hard to envisage. Farmers need to get a decent price for producing decent food. Where possible we must establish more direct links between producers and consumers – whether through organic box schemes, local purchasing, or fair trade schemes nationally as well as internationally. Government intervention is needed to stabilise prices, to guarantee food security, to make loans available to farmers so they are not forced to sell when the harvest comes in and prices are at their lowest, to enable a new generation to be able to afford to enter farming.

But all this pales into insignificance compared with the need to challenge and curb the power of agribusiness, the overwhelming beneficiary of both US and EU subsidy regimes. Simply trying to restore market mechanisms in agriculture is no solution, as the US experience shows so vividly. It just hastens the process of concentration in an already rottenly concentrated sector. It is time to think afresh and to ally ourselves with small farmer movements throughout the world in their demands for support and protection for small farmers and their wider organisations, Confederation Paysanne Européenne and Via Campesina. They will be making their voices heard in the current rounds of discussion on the WTO Agreement on Agriculture. They need support against those who would maintain the status quo or those who want 'more market' and 'less regulation'. Regulation is the only way to curb the power of agribusiness and to save a non-industrial, non-Taylorised view of how our food can be produced – and our natural world conserved.

6 Towards a solidaristic citizens' and farmers' CAP

The Confédération Paysanne's proposals provide a profound challenge to the processes that create exclusion in the rural milieu. The first priority is the absolute necessity of maintaining the present number of farm units in Europe. For the Confédération Paysanne, the fabric of small and medium-sized farms which knit together the lands of Europe is the only guarantee of an agriculture that both respects the environment and can provide a diversity of foodstuffs. Though a minority presence in the rural world today, the presence of such an agriculture remains a fundamental element in the durability of social life in rural areas. Every farm that disappears is another sign of the failure of the CAP. Rural employment must be the pillar on which a new CAP is built, because there cannot be a sustainable agriculture if the number of farm units continues to fall as predicted.

End the supposed export vocation of the EU

For reasons already mentioned, the EU must abandon its sacrosanct vocation to feed the world. Without the subsidies given to producers in the North, world markets for primary agricultural produce will never be profitable for European farmers. To continue this headlong rush to assault world markets is to accept the total deregulation of economies and the sustained domination of rich countries over the countries of the South.

Of course, the EU should not abandon all its exports. It is a matter of choosing which to foster: several of its agricultural products with a high added value are among the world's finest: wines and spirits, foie gras, cheeses and the like, expressing as they do the value of real *savoir faire* as well as of a real local economy. These exports must be maintained and developed without subsidies. On the other hand, it is irresponsible to insist on exporting basic produce such as milk powder, cereals, poultry and cheap cuts of red meat to a market fed by the surpluses of the large producer countries (the USA, Canada) or by the output of countries having an agriculture modelled on ranching or latifundianism (Australia, New Zealand, Latin America). These products will never be competitive on the world market without specific export or domestic subsidies

There is clearly a place for an intelligent protectionism – something that lies between a narrow nationalism and an unbridled globalisation. What needs to be built is a political and institutional structuring of exchanges on an appropriate regional scale and between countries at similar levels of development.

Contrary to what the defenders of liberalisation of trade affirm, giving up their export vocation – at least for those products which are not competitive on the world market without special subsidy – is the least dangerous option for Europe's farmers. From within the EU, as we shall show, an overall supply management of what is produced is the indispensable tool for matching supply to internal demand. It must be stressed that this scenario is not beyond political bounds. It certainly does demand an EU about-turn, but it is the only way of bringing general agreement among the various parties in the rest of the world. It could be acceptable and beneficial to developing countries, since the EU would be eliminating its destabilising low-price exports, and could even use all or part of the money received from variable levies on imports to sustain a development fund for the agricultures of the South. It would be equally acceptable to the USA and the Cairns Group of countries, who would view very favourably an undertaking by the EU to stop its enormous exports of cereals (25 million tonnes) and of meat (1.5 million tonnes). With such undertakings, these countries would be far more ready to agree to accept a restriction of access to the European market.

The EU would then be in a strong position to uphold the rights of other countries or groups of countries to defend their frontiers. It is in protecting their agricultures in this way – in order to develop their self-sufficiency and food security, both quantitatively and qualitatively, with respect for others' cultural and dietary choices – that countries could respond best to the expectations of their peoples and to the needs of their farmers.

Box 6.1: The protein plan: 'food sovereignty' in place of 'export vocation'

Establishing a 'protein plan' would be an important step towards challenging the export vocation of the European Union. Europe devotes around 6 to 7 million hectares to oilseed and protein crops and imports the output of more than 16 million hectares (principally in the USA, Brazil and Argentina) for animal feed – the equivalent of half the total agricultural area in use in France! A precondition of any internal policy aiming to reduce the EU's vegetable protein dependence is the establishment of some mechanism to protect the EU's own output from these duty-free imports. The EU, rather than opening its doors ever wider to the cargoes of genetically modified soya coming from the USA and Brazil, must make this rebalancing a priority.

There are two aspects to this:

First, increase the area devoted to growing oilseed and protein crops

The EU's current dependence on imported proteins could be halved by, first, planting and cultivating non-intensively the fields that currently lie fallow – around 4 million hectares – and, second, reconverting the fields currently devoted to cereals for export – another 4 to 5 million hectares.

Any such plan would have to respect a balanced crop rotation as well as ensuring a wide geographical spread of these new crops over the whole of the European farming area to avoid (in the desire to make animal-rearing self-sufficient) favouring the areas which currently specialise in field crops on a large scale.

Second, reduce the EU's consumption of proteins

Consumption of proteins in Europe exploded with the growing of maize for silage and the development of white-meat production on an industrial scale. Regaining independence in proteins must involve a significant reduction in the amount used for stock rearing. Breeders must be encouraged to produce and consume their own proteins, principally grasses and leguminous plants for ruminants. The imbalance between silage maize and grass must be rectified by the creation of a bonus devoted to the production of fodder crops.

Supply management

The second aspect of challenging the policies pursued up till now follows from the first. To be coherent, giving up the principle of Europe as exporter entails opposing the orientation of the CAP to the world market and thus managing supply.

That is why the various Common Marketing regimes must be substantially reformed and tools for managing supply put in place by means of plans to limit output per worker.

Today, all produce for which prices have remained adequate is subject to regulation of supply. Many *appellation contrôlée* vineyards impose maximum production limits in order to balance supply and demand. The framework for controlling milk production has also helped impede a drift towards over-production and a collapse in prices, even if the Confédération Paysanne does not accept the unjust division of the rights to produce. But this regulation has been called into question once again by the Berlin Agreement which envisages the elimination of milk quotas around 2006.

On the contrary, European supply must adapt to internal demand. Making this happen would amount to a complete overthrow of the current regime, which operates essentially by an incessant withdrawal of farmers from farming.

That is why, when many products today – beef above all – are drowning in excess output, it has become essential to adjust output to internal demand. The appropriate response to structural over-production, whose destructive effects on both farmers and society we are well aware of, is quantitative supply management, with the exception of those products that are competitive without direct subsidies, export restitutions or protection against imports (which is generally the case with high value-added goods).

This regulation can only be socially acceptable if it is associated with a redistribution of production among farmers and countries. It can be summed up in the proposition:'There aren't too many producers, but there are producers who produce too much.' From this flows the need to attribute rights to produce that take account of the number of active workers on the farm. These rights would also have to be apportioned between regions and countries, taking into account what different areas are naturally suited to and what has been produced historically in order to give each country a quota that allows it to maintain its existing farmers, or even to increase their number.

A policy founded on equitable prices

At first sight, consumers might have believed that the 1992 reforms, which reduced intervention prices, would increase their purchasing power. The concomitant evolution of the indices of farm gate and of retail food prices led to rapid disenchantment: from 1990 to 1998 the former fell by 11.1 per cent while the latter rose by 10.7 per cent The tendency was the same in the USA, where the price of a food basket rose by 2.8 per cent in real terms from 1986 to 1998 while the value received for the agricultural produce at the farm gate fell by 35.7 per cent The conclusion is inevitable: agribusiness and the large distributors did not pass the fall in agricultural prices onto the consumer.

Not only that. The consumer/taxpayer had to pay twice at the same time, not just to finance agricultural support but also to meet the costs of cleaning up the pollution arising from a number of intensive farming practices.

Once again we must stress that the cost of the primary agricultural produce contained in the final product that is purchased in the supermarkets is indeed marginal. Confirming this reality, Commissioner Fischler recently declared at the height of the argument about the CAP that a rise of 15 per cent in agricultural prices would only lead to a 2 per cent increase in cost of the household basket.

What exactly are world prices? Defenders of free trade say they are real prices that set an appropriate baseline. The truth, as we have already shown clearly (see Chapter 1), is quite different. Over and above the fact that they concern only a minimal part of world production (6–10 per cent for cereals, milk and meat products), they are totally unrelated to the real costs of production and are largely financed by the taxpayer. To win markets and impose their produce on the countries of the South, firms lower their prices drastically – and raise them again when local produce has been eliminated.

What do we mean by equitable prices? It is a question of prices that cover the costs of production, remuneration of the farmer's labour and the multifunctional role of agriculture at one and the same time. Far from being a corporatist (i.e. narrow, self-interested) demand, this insistence on the reality of prices goes to the heart of what society wants. We know the damage caused by a frenetic search for the lowest possible costs of production, whether at the level of public health (and the scandal of contaminated feedstuffs is there as a constant reminder), the destruction of the social fabric or the damage caused to the environment. Why then the crazy search for the lowest possible prices when it comes to the very food we consume?

To guarantee such prices, the EU must accept the logic of regulating imports because these, as we know, can be particularly destabilising. From this perspective there is a need to re-establish the right to impose 'variable levies' on imports, suppressed in the wake of the Marrakech Agreement, levies which vary in relation to the differential between European and world prices. Of course that is not enough: to support the remuneration of family and farm work, equitable prices have to be guaranteed, but only up to a certain level of output per active worker on the farm.

Equitable prices would be based on those of the most favoured regions and a safety net be guaranteed by the state in the event of a crisis, that is when prices fall below the costs of production (including farmers' remuneration). In this event a compensatory mechanism must allow affected farms to receive a price supplement up to a certain level. And, pursuing the logic of solidarity, the large distributors and agri-food industries would appear to be by far the best placed to shell out the funds necessary to establish such a scheme via some tax mechanism.

It is *not* a question of falling back into the old system of guaranteeing prices whatever the level of output. The times when, at every crisis, society is called on to fork out exceptional (until the next time!) and unfairly shared aid must be consigned to the past. What is called for is a real contract between farmers and society, taking into account support to the least-favoured regions where costs of production are naturally higher because of farming and climatic factors. Some mechanism of price support is needed, but always limited to a certain output per active worker.

It is both necessary and urgent to establish some anti-crisis national regulatory tools while waiting for such a market policy to be put in place. The successive crises which have washed over agriculture in recent years are a resounding refutation of the claimed redistributive effects of the free market. Some prices paid to producers have even fallen below the institutional prices fixed by the CAP, without consumers benefiting in the slightest. It is clear that the market is incapable of managing an optimal allocation of wealth. The reality is that any margins are shared out in favour of the dominant actors, that is to say the transnational wholesalers and the agri-food industry.[1] This is even more true in times of crisis, and where distribution is more closely integrated with production (as is the case with the pork, poultry and fish).

Today, two systems stand in opposition: agribusiness which uses the process of increasing concentration to maximise the profits of its shareholders, and small, often family, businesses in the artisanal and agricultural sectors which suffer the consequences of these practices and see their capacity to produce wealth constantly being eroded as they struggle to survive.

As a result public powers are faced with a choice: to favour the interests of agribusiness, which wants to get its inputs at the lowest prices possible; or to take care of the farmers who are victims of one crisis after another (pork, poultry, fruit and vegetables, rabbit, beef, lamb...)

The regular fall in intervention prices exposes farmers constantly to the effects of price fluctuation. Faced with this, many countries have already adopted schemes of income insurance which farmers may subscribe to. The USA has had such programmes since 1996 and they are currently being developed in Europe. Since 1999, English cereal farmers have been able to subscribe to the first revenue insurance scheme in Europe, guaranteeing 90 per cent of the ten-year average of the regional return over the previous decade multiplied by 95 per cent of the rate quoted on the London forward market...

Superficially seductive, it is necessary to bear in mind that those subscribing to such a scheme must have the means to do so, since such insurance does not come cheap. And if small farmers in Europe cannot afford it, what about small farmers in Africa? Furthermore, the dangers and consequences of dumping remain since this system encourages a fall in prices. And, in as much as such a system takes the market price of wheat as its reference point (whether the forward market in London or very often that in Chicago), these are the places where the famous world market price is constructed which, as we have already argued, has no substantive meaning.

In order to ensure equitable prices are actually paid, the problem of marketing 'primary' agricultural produce and of the relations between producers and distributors has also to be addressed. A clear and quick method of arbitrating between the different interests is essential. In effect, the ever-increasing concentration of distribution, the aggressive commercial practices of the large shops and the one-sided domination that the large distributors exercise in relation to the producers often impose unacceptable social and economic burdens on the latter. One must find voluntary ways of re-establishing the transparency and integrity of transactions.

To guarantee a balanced relationship and an equitable distribution of the profit margins among producers, the processors and the large distributors would have to encourage quality production and contribute to a real policy of spatial planning, linked among other things to the development of local markets and local trade.

A de-intensified agriculture

If we want to respond to the legitimate demands of consumers, the environmental stakes and the demand for the maintenance of employment in farming, we cannot avoid profound changes in certain methods of production. For years the regulation of supply within the framework of the CAP has been achieved solely by reducing the number of farmers and by not replacing them with new ones, on the basis of a competition among ever more modernised – and indebted – farmers.

To maintain the current number of farmers, we must produce less but better. A CAP reformed on a new basis would have to engage in de-intensification of agriculture as quickly as possible. It must be stressed from the outset that this proposal has nothing whatsoever to do with 'extensification' (that is, each farmer producing as much as is produced now but on a larger area). Such a policy would merely empty Europe of its farmers, while filling the land with herds reared in a very extensive way. On the contrary, in order to maintain a healthy population of farmers on the land, the de-intensification of production must express itself in a reduction in the output of each producer, the only way of avoiding the coexistence of fallow fields and intensively-farmed lands side by side. This new regulation of supply would in the first instance call into question the totality of industrial practices in agriculture: the massive consumption of additives, the utilisation of antibiotics and of growth hormones, animals brought up in concentration-camp conditions, growing high-return but poor-quality wheat, intensive fattening of cattle and so on. It is a safe bet that on this issue the agri-food interests would be opposed to the general aspirations of farmers and of society!

This sustainable agriculture, which keeps the countryside peopled and respects natural balances, already exists as we have seen: it is a 'sustainable small farming' (*l'agriculture paysanne*). Many farmers already practice it, against the current of the CAP, often without even knowing it. To generalise this form of agriculture, new tools are needed.

A genuine policy of rural development

A genuine policy of rural development must be created out of a new agricultural policy which goes beyond support for agriculture, to the revitalisation of the rural world.

The political logic has to be changed. Europe must cease privileging the holy trinity of enlargement, concentration and industrialisation, and instead put small farms back into the heart of agriculture where their role at the centre of the rural world is irreplaceable. Favouring non-enlargement in place of enlargement is the precondition for the sustainability of small farmers' agriculture. A standard subsidy targeted on small farms and attributed to each person working on them would encourage the limiting of production within agreed limits, in order to economise on the means of production while simultaneously maximising returns. A measure of this kind would be an excellent response to the entry of the CEEC countries into the EU, just as it would give a boost to the redistribution of public subsidies to the benefit of the countries of southern Europe. The introduction of a policy that privileges equitable prices is in itself insufficient to ensure the durability of millions of very small farms in the future Europe of 25.

Making small farming sustainable is not enough: we must also support both agricultural and artisanal start-ups in the rural milieu. The problem of starting up today is posed in new ways. On the one hand, new start-ups are vital to maintain social cohesion in the countryside, of which agriculture is a major factor; but on the other hand the institutional framework for supporting new installations is bankrupt in France, and not much better elsewhere. Having based their criteria for access to land on a productivist model, existing institutions are now incapable of compensating for the departure of so many farmers. In parallel to this failure from above, a movement has developed from the bottom up: of installations called 'progressive', projects 'outside the norms' which are 'carried through not only by young people from agricultural backgrounds but also by people from urban, and often unemployed, backgrounds.'[2] Advocates of a radical alternative to the dominant model, these newly installed people generally practice a small family agriculture that can be described at one and the same time as a 'local agriculture' (processing and sale in a small area) and a 'solidaristic agriculture', so important are the links which bind them to other non-agricultural actors in their local regions.[3]

These start-ups, of which the numbers grow year by year and which in some cases have now began to exceed those favoured by the system, do not benefit from any subsidies. Too innovatory! A reform is urgently called for, with perhaps the awarding of a career grant, repayable when one quits the project. This would also place a brake on the capitalist drift that one sees today in Europe towards a massive indebtedness that makes new start-ups in the rural milieu ever more hazardous.

[107]

The land question

Regulating access to land is essential to preserve the fabric of small and medium farms which still knit the countryside of Europe together. Currently, withdrawals from farming are not nearly being made good by new entrants. To take the case of France, each year sees the disappearance of around 4 per cent of farm units. Behind this gross figure there are some quite disturbing developments: from 1967 to 1997 the average agricultural area in use of French farms increased by 140 per cent. The 1992 CAP reform, subsidising hectares rather than produce, accelerated the trend to land concentration, the premise of an industrial-type agriculture. The larger the farming units, the faster they grow. We see today in France that 2 per cent of farming units, those of over 200 hectares, make up 14 per cent of the agricultural area in use.[4] The trends elsewhere in the EU are much the same. It is virtually impossible to pass these units on to new farmers, however, because they demand a level of capitalisation beyond the reach of most new entrants.

In contrast, there is great competition among those who want to enter farming. Among the many factors that make it more and more different for candidates wishing to start up to find the land of their dreams are the tentacular growth of villages, gnawing little by little into better agriculture land, and the multiplication of tourist uses for land (from the creation of golf courses to renting out land for private hunts, running through competition from hotel or skiing infrastructures etc). All these activities are much more profitable for the owner of the land than a small agricultural holding.

To create jobs it is necessary to liberate land and to open up access to it substantially: from Brazil to Europe, agrarian reform is on the agenda.

Giving answers to farmers while awaiting CAP reform

Capping and modulating subsidies

We know today that direct subsidies will not go away at the wave of a wand, however much the Confédération Paysanne wants their disappearance in favour of equitable prices. At the same time, the skewed distribution of existing public subsidies in agriculture is a permanent trade-union challenge facing the Confédération Paysanne and its sister unions.

If a monopoly of 80 per cent of subsidies by the 20 per cent of largest farmers is still the norm throughout the EU, the European Court of Auditors has at least condemned the way in which 4 per cent of the large cereal producers receive 40 per cent of the subsidies! For the Confédération Paysanne, capping and modulating (redistributing) subsidies is an eminently political question and should not be treated in a budgetary and technical manner.

While awaiting a policy which favours equitable prices, such capping and modulation should have two principal objectives: first, to reduce the incentives to enlarge farms, and to make funds available for a policy of redistribution in favour of small farms; and second, to encourage quality and respect for the environment.

While the Berlin Agreement closed the door to capping subsidies, it none the less gave member states the option of modulating them by up to 20 per cent of their value.

The introduction of this measure in France was unfortunately not in accordance with the objectives that the Confédération Paysanne would have assigned to it: the principal criterion of modulation is in effect the level of aid. But high levels of subsidy in no way guarantee a high income for the farmer For example, sheep farmers receive high subsidies but remain among the poorest of farmers, while large milk or beet producers who receive subsidies for cereals ought to have these much more significantly reduced because of their overall profitability. That is not what happens in practice: the subsidies to a milk producer with a quota of 350,000 litres and an area eligible for subsidy of 75 hectares, say, are not modulated, while those of a farmer in an intermediate area with 150 hectares of field crops, are.

An effective modulation policy must improve the basic level of aid per active worker, support farming units of modest size more strongly and discourage any enlargement that does not create jobs. It must also avoid as far as possible the effects of thresholds that push people towards reaching the next level, which is taken as the norm, and that encourage getting around the rules by a fictitious division of the farm. This capping would apply to the totality of subsidies given, taking everything produced into account, and would be decided upon mainly in relation to the economic size of the farm per active worker.

Introducing social criteria for subsidies

A significant part of the budgets devoted to agriculture in Europe, whether they come form the EU or from the member states or local collectivities, serves only to reinforce the industrial systems of agriculture or to plaster over the damage wreaked by productivism. As is well known, the productivist system destroys agricultural employment and at the same time is very often a major employer of precarious/insecure labour for short periods. So a farm unit of more than 1,000 hectares of peaches in the Bouches-du-Rhône department in France would resort to the short-term use of more than 80 foreign workers under contract, lodged in caravans and living in generally deplorable conditions.

The Confédération Paysanne perceives an urgent need to introduce social criteria into agricultural support so as to discourage such systems of production. All subsidies to agriculture, whether direct subsidies to marketing or structural ones (for investment, start-up etc.), whatever their source, must be conditional on respect for criteria relating to employment in order to encourage an agriculture which employs proportionally more labour per unit of output and respects dignified social norms.

Reinforcing cross-compliance

Cross-compliance refers to supports of whatever kind that are given within an ecologically-based framework. The model of 'always produce more' is less and less socially acceptable. To the health crises of recent years must be added the increasingly acute perception of the effects of intensive agriculture on the environment. In this regard, the reforms of 1992 and 1999 have only amplified the negative effects of agriculture. Paradoxically, those systems of agriculture that benefit most from the current CAP regime also cause the greatest environmental damage.

A small number of farmers often evade environmental legislation entirely – a situation that is prejudicial to their profession and to society in general. In France – as elsewhere – the state bears a responsibility for the failure to enforce the law. It was the company Lyonnaise des Eaux against whom consumers first turned in outrage for the pollution of water in the region of Guincamp. But the administrative tribunal of Rennes – and this was a first – found that the state had failed in its duty to prevent pollution from nitrates of agricultural origin and did not control units using factory-farm methods of animal rearing. It recognised the Ministry of the Environment as responsible and ordered it to recompense the company.

We can see also the weakness of French and European regulations, particularly concerning pesticides, where the public powers are often manipulated by continuous pressure from the agri-pharmaceutical transnationals. The derisory impact of taxes and pollution charges employed recently under the 'polluter-pays' principle make the regulations totally unenforceable. The chief culprit is the CAP itself. Despite moving from a policy of price support to one of direct subsidies, it has maintained the same emphasis of encouraging and favouring quantity over quality. Not every farmer is a polluter by a long chalk, but what is intolerable is that the CAP helps those who use polluting production methods more than it does others; nowhere is this truer than in the environmental effects of maize production discussed earlier.

Just as all public aid to agriculture must be socially conditional and the quality of produce encouraged and protected from the vicissitudes of the market, so too must public support of whatever kind be given within an ecologically based framework. The baseline must be respect for environmental regulations: those already in place and those which, according to the local and natural conditions, are needed to fulfil clearly defined objectives for the protection or restoration of the quality of the natural resources. This schema, compulsory for every farmer, must not prevent the establishment of temporary localised contracts, freely engaged in by farmers, who wish to fix a *higher* level of objectives.

7 Conclusion

To be a player in the future of agriculture, to contribute to writing a new page in its history, and to do it with all those who are concerned with social, and environmental issues, or those who care about what food lands on our plates; these are the challenges that the Confédération Paysanne is taking up with the help of others. The battles lost in advance are those no one dares to lead, whether from the inertia of fatalism or the pressure of monolithic thinking. The militants of the Conf haven't hesitated to break the law in a legitimate cause. We would have been ashamed *not* to have dismantled a McDonald's when our quality produce was sanctioned in retaliation for the refusal to import US beef fed with hormones. Not to have destroyed GMO trials in open fields which contaminate neighbouring plots, in the name of the precautionary principle, would have made us collaborators. While in the USA some 40 million hectares of GMO crops will inevitably bring about cross-breeding with a whole host of plants and modify nature in an irreversible way with incalculable consequences, the European struggle of farmers, consumers and environmentalists allows us to say that we have put the issue of GMOs high on the public agenda.

Now the struggle we must spearhead is one for a different Common Agricultural Policy. To succeed we must identify and label our adversaries: those who advance their interests barefacedly, like the agri-chemical companies selling fertilisers and pesticides which France is world champion at consuming, and the seed companies striving to control life through means ranging from the genetic engineering of new life forms to the patenting of animals, plants and micro-organisms. There are complicities which tend to make their system of production unassailable; complicities between public and private research which reinforce one another with capital and with monopolistic discoveries; complicities also within the agricultural profession, where public subsidies are used by the large beneficiaries to prop up an elitist, produc-tivist system, as cheques for millions of euros are gleefully cashed. There are perhaps political complicities as well: witness the French parliamentary colloquium on food secu-rity, organised by the Senate in November 1999, sponsored by Aventis and Dupont de Nemours!

Just as it is essential to expose the activities of our adver-saries, so it is urgent to mobilise all our allies, whether in agreement or yet to be convinced of the indissoluble links among social, environmental and quality-of-food issues and cultural identity in its broadest sense. The maintenance of a significant number of farmers in France and throughout Europe is the *sine qua non* of sustainable, small farming practices which would allow us to guarantee food worthy of the name. We must avoid the pitfall of a seductive but dangerous green liberalism or of making some subsidies dependent on 'respectable' environmental practices as an acceptable response. If we accept that, the countryside will become a non-polluted desert, but a desert none the less. To maintain a significant agricultural population requires that farmers derive an income from the sale of their produce and not from subsidies. To maintain stability of agricultural prices, production has to be organised with the rules of the game spelled out clearly in order to avoid the creation of destructive surpluses. This quantitative control means call-ing into question all intensive and industrial processes of production and spreading a sustainable small farmers' agri-culture that is both more economically viable and more autonomous. Militant farmers are already putting such alternative practices into effect, with greater or lesser difficulty because they go against the grain of policies that do not support an independent agriculture. A large number of consumers have already made the choice of quality food from organic agriculture or quality labels.

However welcome, these beginnings of a radical alternative are insufficient. To stop here would be to ratify the existence of a dual-track agriculture and an associated dual-quality food. Junk food (*malbouffe*) for the less socially advantaged and the clearly disadvantaged would coexist with niche quality food for the comfortable classes. We will not accept such a perspective.

We must therefore advance together on the platform of a different agricultural policy with a global perspective. 'Alliance' is the word chosen by the Confédération Paysanne to describe its work with other consumer, environmental or social organisations. We must enlarge and extend our alliances to include all those who raise questions about the way their food is produced. That is the goal the Conf has set itself. Nothing less will suffice.

Appendix 1. *L'agriculture paysanne*: a charter for small farming

L'agriculture paysanne or 'small farming' is an agriculture that both respects the farmer and responds to society's expectations.

The raison d'être of small farming is to promote an agriculture that responds effective to of society's needs for:

- Food: consumers increasingly demand food that is both tastier and healthier. They want to know how their food is produced.
- Rural development: until the 1950s the farming population represented more than half the rural population, animating and providing the rhythm of rural life.
- The goods and services produced by agriculture that relate to quality of life, the countryside and the management of rural space.
- Things relating to the quality and diversity of the environment, that is, concerning the ecological function of agriculture.

In response to these needs, agriculture produces goods that are marketable (both food and non-food commodities) and non-marketable (countryside, territory, environment). Small farming produces both categories of goods with the quality demanded at the same time. It is thus a refusal of a dual or a two-speed agriculture, dedicated on the one hand to exporting and on the other to fulfilling the functions of preserving rural space.

Small farming embodies three aspects, all of which are equally fundamental:

- It has a social dimension based on employment, solidarity among farmers, regions and farmers of the world. Respect for every farmer and every region's right to produce is fundamental, otherwise the more powerful will trample on others' right to life, a token neither of equilibrium nor or humanity. Small farming allows a maximum number of active workers to exercise the profession of agriculture.
- It has to be economically effective. It must create added value in relation to the means of production employed and the quantities produced. That is the precondition for farmers to live off relatively modest volumes of production, the precondition for maintaining a large number of active people in the field. This economically effective production goes hand in hand with quality production.
- It must respect both consumers and nature. This is the obligatory counterpart to the contribution the collectivity makes to the agricultural sector. It is a question here of food quality, ecological equilibrium, countryside, biodiversity and the like.

Taking these different dimensions into account depends on the personal choices of farmers (this incorporates the idea of individual responsibility) but also on the political framework. Agricultural policy, through its choices, favours or handicaps the development of this type of farming.

Small farming is defined by an 'approach' (*une*

'*démarche*') and by 'boundary conditions' (*un 'périmetre'*), two terms which continually crop up in the Confédération Paysanne's discussions on the topic. These two dimensions are unavoidable and complementary. The approach is the direction, the compass, the goal, the point on the horizon one is aiming for, whatever the realities on the ground. It is crucial because it represents the ongoing driving force that motivates both individuals and groups. It is ongoing because there are always challenges to surmount, contradictions to resolve, equilibria to find. In the Charter this approach is concretised in the 'Ten principles of small family farming'.

The moment society's demands on agriculture become more and more precise, the moment conflicts erupt between the general public and a certain type of agriculture, it becomes essential to define precisely the contours of the agriculture society wants in exchange for the public subsidies it is paying out. If we want to limit intensification, we must define a maximum level of nitrogen per hectare, a maximum size of enterprise per active worker and so on. The sphere of concerns or the 'boundary conditions' for small farming are set by these wider considerations.

The development of small farming depends on two conditions. First is a policy framework that, instead of encouraging concentration and industrialised agriculture, can and should sustain small family farming. The second relates to the individual choices of the farmers on their farms; here we have a space for initiatives and taking responsibility.

The production of this Charter is an important and novel event. Its utility is found at a number of levels:

- It can be used to formulate policy proposals for agriculture (CAP reform, formulae for social or ecological conditionality etc.).

- It allows a complete analysis of the farm unit and reveals priority areas for implementing changes.
- It can be used as a tool in education, preparation for new entrants and for reflection on what has been achieved.

Above all this the Charter puts small farming back centre stage at a time when everyone claims to promote sustainable agriculture but when this is so often reduced to nothing more than taking certain environmental considerations into account.

Small farming must allow for a maximum number of farmers spread over the whole countryside to live decently from their craft by producing healthy food of quality, on a farming unit of a human scale, without calling tomorrow's natural resources into question. It must work with the citizenry to make the rural milieu a living milieu, with a framework of life valued by all.

The ten principles of small farming

1. Redistribute output to allow the greatest number of people to become farmers and to be able to earn a living by farming.

Industrialisation and the accompanying concentration of farm units allows production with an ever-decreasing number of workers. In a context where the total quantities needed are globally limited, the development of some is at the expense of others. The right to produce is at the same time the right to work and the right to an income. To allow access of the largest possible number to the craft, the redistribution of the right to produce is a fundamental principle. The state must intervene to organise production and to set the framework for the market. Farmers are partly responsible for the scale of their economic activity. They can work towards a redistribution of production or feed the process of concentration.

2. Show solidarity with the small farmers of other region of Europe and of the world.

Each farmer in the world is, for all the others, 'another farmer in the world'. People can see themselves in competition with all the others or, alternatively, in solidarity and complementary. An agricultural policy which extols aggression on the world's markets where production is in surplus and protectionism for those where there is a shortage, reinforces competition among the world's farmers and ultimately the disappearance of a goodly number of them. Small farming rests on solidarity, and is itself based on two main principles: the right of every people and state in the world to organise its own food security, and thus to protect its agriculture; and the right of all farmers within every state to be involved in production and in the food security of their country.

3. Respect nature.

To produce goods, agriculture uses living and fragile physical elements of the natural world: water, soil, air. These elements which make up the tools of farmers are the property of all. They do not belong to us in our capacity as farmers; they are not the property of our generation. These natural elements must be preserved in order to ensure their durability for use by future generations. 'We don't inherit the earth from our parents, we borrow it from our children.'

4. Make the most of resources which are abundant and husband those that are rare.

Agriculture produces by putting certain elements into motion: soil, air, energy, labour, capital, space. Some of these are abundant and renewable, others are rare and non-renewable. Small farming adapts its approach to the context in terms of climate and soil. It makes the most of what is abundant and renewable and economises on resources that are rare and non-renewable, as far as this is possible. For example, human labour, carried out under socially acceptable conditions, is an abundant resource while the substitution of labour by capital often requires a large amount of often non-renewable energy.

5. Seek transparency in purchasing, production and sale of agricultural products.

Each citizen, each citizen-consumer, has the right to follow the progress of any food product from its production through the stages of transformation until its sale. This means not only being informed but also being able to verify the truth of the information about how the finished product has been produced. This demand for transparency applies to each link in the chain whatever the nature of the production or the networks concerned.

6. Ensure the quality and health value of products.

The quality of any product results fundamentally from the method of production: scale of production, level of intensity, methods of growing or rearing, external inputs. Quality is not subjective. On the contrary, it should be officially recognised and be identifiable and verifiable by every citizen. (Currently there are four measures of quality in France, based upon respect for certain specified conditions: *appelations* (AOCs), AB (agriculture biologique, or organic agriculture), farm labels and certificates of conformity.)

7. Aim for maximum autonomy in the way farms are run.

To be autonomous is at the same time to be in control of ones choices and to have the means of exercising this capacity. The autonomy of farmers rests on their autonomy of decision-making. This is determined by their technical and economic independence. But autonomy is not autarchy. Autarchy leads to isolation and thus to the disappearance of farmers. In contrast, autonomy is based on the partnership and complementarity among products, among farmers, among agricultural regions and among local actors.

8. Seek partnerships with other actors in the rural world.

Agriculture is not a world apart and must not become a world apart. To be viable and socially acceptable, agricultural activity must be part of wider social and economic life. Through the privileged relations it has with the natural world, it can be a place of welcome, of integration and of regional equity. To take part in the dynamic of local life and the rural milieu, agriculture must develop partnerships with other areas of activity, In the same way as small farming can never be divorced from the land, it can never be abstracted from the area in which it is located. Farmers have a responsibility, following from their individual choices, to ensure that these localities develop in a socially and economically balanced and sustainable fashion.

9. Maintain the diversity of both animals bred and plants cultivated.

Highly diverse animal and plant populations are part of humankind's heritage. We have to conserve this biodiversity for many reasons:

- for historical reasons, because we do not have the right to stop the history of life which enriches itself over the course of generations

- for economic reasons, because hundreds of varieties and species are particularly adapted to our regions and our soils.

In the same way as with the land, we can say that we borrow biodiversity from those who will follow us. We must pass it on, enriched.

10. Always think long-term and globally.

It is at the global level that we can grasp the social, economic and environmental aspects of small farming. If one of these aspects is lacking, it is no longer small farming. Small farming corresponds to the ensemble of these ten principles, because the principles are interdependent. None of them in isolation makes up small farming. Each principle is a necessary but not a sufficient condition of what we mean by small farming. Even if it is difficult to take them all into account at the same time, there is a need to have a global vision based on these principles.

Appendix 2. Campaign for an immediate change in the direction of the CAP

The document reproduced here, launched on 12 December 2002, sets out a common position, initiated and developed by the following organisations:

Consumers' organisations
Union nationale des associations familiales (UNAF)
Alliance paysans écologistes consommateurs

Environmental protection and sustainable development organisations
4D – Dossiers et débats pour le développement durable
Les Amis de la terre
Association pour la création de la fondation René Dumont
Réseau action climat France
Réseau Cohérence

Farmers' organisations
Jeunes agriculteurs
Confédération Paysanne
Chrétiens dans le monde rural (CMR)
Mouvement rural de jeunesse chrétienne (MRJC)

International solidarity organisations

Coordination sud

Centre de recherche et d'information pour le développement (CRID)

Comité français pour la solidarité internationale (CFSI)

Groupe catholique contre la faim et pour le développement (CCFD)

Solagral

Groupe de recherche et d'échanges technologiques (GRET)

Afrique vert

Agir ici pour une monde solidaire

Centre international de coopération pour le développement agricole (CICDA)

Fédération artisans du monde

Forum des organisations de solidarité internationale issues des migrations (FORIM)

Solidarité

Another 19 French organisations supported the platform when it was launched.

> We call for an immediate change in the direction of the CAP so that it encourages and guarantees, in Europe and the wider world:
>
> - the right to food sovereignty and respect for small farmers' agriculture
> - equitable prices and employment for farmers
> - healthy food, available to all
> - preservation of the environment, of resources and of natural habitats.
>
> The CAP, an element in European integration that has allowed an improvement in the food self-sufficiency of the 15 member states, is at a turning point. It is currently under attack, both from within and outside the European Union (EU).

Successive food-safety crises, doubts about the quality of agribusiness products, the disappearance of small producers in Europe, the persistence of hunger in poor countries, the degradation of environmental resources (climate, water, soil, biodiversity) – all these are the consequences of the drive to reduce production costs as far as possible. This is evidence of the absurdity of the way the CAP is oriented and shows the need to bring it into line with Community goals relating to sustainable development: international cooperation and solidarity, town and country planning, environmental protection, job creation, the struggle against the greenhouse effect and so on.

The EU of the 15 currently contains 7 million farmers. Its enlargement in 2004 to the 4.5 million farmers of the ten countries of central and eastern Europe assumes a common vision of the CAP and of the resources at its disposal [which it does not have]. In addition, the EU cannot justify to other countries, particularly the poorest, or to public opinion worldwide, the maintenance of a system that generates surpluses that are dumped on the internal markets of other countries. The defence-at-any-cost of export restitutions has provoked an anti-CAP front that has paradoxically spared the USA although that country, while extolling a totally free-market economy, subsidises its agriculture just as extensively. These policies contribute to the impoverishment of small farmers: 600 million of them suffer from hunger worldwide.

The proposals of the Commission, just like the decision of the European Council to maintain the current budget for agricultural support and direct subsidies until 2006, does not address the crucial question of how agricultural prices are fixed and allows the practice of dumping – the sale of agricultural products on external markets at prices below cost – to continue.

We, supporting organisations, representing numerous activists in civil society affected by this economic, social, environmental and health dumping, demand:

Equitable agricultural prices and social policies to maintain and to create jobs and economic activity.
The fall of prices, bringing with it a fall in the income of producers, is a cause of food insecurity and rural exodus in the South. In the North it pushes countries to spend ever more on supporting the incomes of producers. The consequences are harmful for the North as well as for the South: 200,000 active farmers disappear each year in Europe and 40 per cent of farmers in France have an income below the minimum wage. Over the past ten years the price of wheat on the internal market in France has been halved. European chicken is sold at €1.37 per kilo in the markets of West Africa while the local cost of production is about €2.28, a situation which ruins the local farmers.

Agricultural income must be based on equitable prices, guaranteed in particular by protecting the internal market and by mechanisms to regulate and redistribute the amounts produced. Only small enterprises and those situated in less-productive zones should have the right to direct subsidies to complement their incomes. The effect of this on consumers would be very limited given the tiny proportion of the final price that is made up by producer costs – most of the price being determined by the margins taken by intermediaries. On top of this, public policies must guarantee access to healthy and sufficient food for all.

Policies to preserve the environment and to produce healthy food for all.
By encouraging productivist systems of production, the orientation of the CAP has led to polluting practices and the production of poor-quality food. Efforts made by small farmers to develop a sustainable agriculture that respects the environment have neither been sufficiently recognized nor encouraged by the current CAP.

Environmental regulations must be respected by all and there must be effective means of inspection and sanctions.

To complement these, voluntary steps in the direction of a sustainable agriculture that give real guarantees to consumers must be supported.

We believe that the current reform proposed by the European Commission does not correspond to these objectives and that the decision of the European Council can only delay the quest for a viable solution, leaving the field free to those who want to dismantle the CAP entirely in the long run.

The change in the direction of the CAP that we are calling for, based on equitable prices, will allow a much higher proportion of the financial resources from the same budget to be used to encourage a sustainable agriculture and a balanced rural development across an enlarged Europe of 25. Moreover, this change in direction will allow the EU to launch a renegotiation of the WTO's Agreement on Agriculture and take steps to reconstitute the system of fixing agricultural world prices, which is the only way to improve the situation of small farmers worldwide.

We, supporting organisations, are ready by our actions in alerting the public and through our contacts with partners in Europe and the world to support the efforts of France and the EU to promote the emergence of a sustainable agriculture.

For that, the CAP must be reformed immediately by implementing the totality of the following measures, which cannot be dissociated from one another:

- the introduction of prices that are equitable in relation to costs of production
- an end to direct or indirect subsidies for exports
- the protection of the European market against imports, and negotiation of special agreements with developing countries as a step towards international solidarity, based upon equitable prices for all parties concerned

- the regulation of quantities produced in order to bring them into line with internal demand
- the equitable redistribution of production, with the goal of maintaining agricultural and rural activities in all of the regions
- the introduction of policies to preserve the environment and to produce healthy food available to all.

This reform of the CAP will allow the EU to throw itself into renegotiating the WTO's Agreement on Agriculture in 2003 with the goal of raising and stabilising world agricultural prices.

- reform in the direction of regulating internal markets, including the prohibition of dumping and respect for the principle of food sovereignty
- the launch of negotiations on new forms of international exchange of produce and of mechanisms to stabilise agriculture prices
- the strengthening of regional zones of agricultural and food sovereignty and the promotion of exchanges within these spaces.

The maintenance of a strong agricultural policy is justified if the EU commits itself to a reform towards sustainable agriculture and if it regulates agricultural output in order to avoid the export of surpluses prejudicial to farmers in other countries. The EU will then legitimately be able to claim the right, for itself and for others, to introduce measures, particularly financial ones, to protect its farmers, its environment and the health of its consumers.

Appendix 3. Resources

A: Farmers' organisation

Confédération Paysanne
81 avenue de la république, 93170 Bagnolet, France
http://www.confederationpaysanne.fr

Coordination Paysanne Européenne (European Farmer Co-ordination) (CPE)
Rue de la Sablonnière 18, 1000 Brussels-Belgium
http://www.cpefarmers.org/en/
CPE consists of 18 farmer and rural organisations from 11 European countries (both members and non members of the EU). It was created in 1986 following European farmers' meetings which had been held annually from 1981.

Its priorities include: many sustainable family farms; economic recognition of farmers' work through the sale of their products, which must represent the major part of their income; sustainable modes of production respecting the quality and safety of the products and care of the environment; supply management; a fair distribution of the public funds between farms, between sectors of production and between regions; balanced production among all the regions of Europe; a relationship of solidarity with the farmers of Central Europe and other continents; and the elimination of dumping in international trade.

In 1993 CPE, together with farmers' organisations from

other continents, took part in the creation of a worldwide farmer movement, Via Campesina.

Via Campesina
Secretaría Operativa, Operative Secretariat Tegucigalpa, Apdo. Postal 3628MDC, Honduras, C.A.
http://www.viacampesina.org/
Via Campesina is an international movement that coordinates peasant organizations of small and middle-scale producers, agricultural workers, rural women, and indigenous communities from Asia, Africa, America, and Europe.

Its first conference was held in Mons, Belgium, in May 1993 where it was constituted as a World Organization, and its first strategic guidelines and structure were defined. Its second international conference in Tlaxcala, Mexico, in April, 1996, was attended by 37 countries and 69 organizations.

It is an autonomous, pluralistic movement, independent from all political, economic, or other denominations. It is integrated by national and regional organizations whose autonomy is respected. Its principal goal is to develop solidarity and unity in the diversity among small farmer organizations, in order to promote economic relations of equality and social justice, the preservation of land, food sovereignty, sustainable agricultural production, and an equality based on small and medium-scale producers.

Via Campesina is organised in eight regions: Europe, Northeast and Southeast Asia, South Asia, North America, the Caribbean, Central America, South America and Africa.

National Family Farm Coalition (NFFC), USA
110 Maryland Ave., N.E., Suite 307, Washington, DC 20002
http://www.nffc.net/
The NFFC was founded in 1986 to serve as a national link for grassroots organisations working on family farm issues in the USA. Membership currently consists of 33 grassroots

farm, resource conservation, and rural advocacy groups from 33 states.

NFFC brings together farmers and others to organise national projects focused on preserving and strengthening family farms. These projects include: the organisation of farmer pricing agencies and true farmer-owned cooperatives; vigorous advocacy for farm and trade policy centred on cost of production plus profit pricing at farm level; environmental stewardship; an affordable food supply; educational campaigns about biotechnology and corporate control of food production; and petition campaigns to repeal mandatory federal producer checkoffs.

It strongly opposes the vertical integration of agriculture, and serves as a network for groups opposing corporate agriculture. NFFC works to promote the safety of the food supply and the security of those who make it possible.

National Farmers Union Canada
2717 Wentz Avenue, Saskatoon, SK S7K – 4B6
http://www.nfu.ca/
The National Farmers Union describes itself as 'farm families sharing common goals. Each family member – farmer, spouse and children, ages 14 to 21 – are full members of the Union and enjoy all rights and privileges within the Union. This structure recognizes that every family member contributes to the farm by working on it, or providing supporting income through off-farm employment.'

It works for agricultural policies which will ensure dignity and security of income for farm families while enhancing the land for future generations.

The Small and Family Farms Alliance (SFFA), UK
E-mail: michael@mhart.fsbusiness.co.uk
The SFFA was formed in 1999 as a coalition of several organisations to give one voice for family farmers in the

UK. It works nationally, within Europe through the Family Farmers' Association which is a member of CPE, and also independently as SFFA, and at an international level with farming and other organisations in many countries, including the USA, Canada and India. SFFA also works with environmentalist, consumer and development NGOs, groups and others on farming and food, and tries to promote a better understanding of agriculture among non-farming people.

Family Farmers' Association (formerly the Small Farmers' Association), UK
Osborne Newton, Aveton Gifford, Kingsbridge, Devon TQ7 4PE
Tel: +44 1548 852794
The association campaigns in favour of family farms. It is farmer-based but encourages a wider public to join: 'If you want farming to do more than produce cheap food, if you are interested in animal welfare, healthy food, and conservation of both the countryside and the rural community – you should join the Family Farmers' Association.'

B: Research and campaigning groups

ActionAid
http://www.actionaid.org/
Founded in 1972, with 88 UK supporters sponsoring 88 children in India and Kenya, Action Aid came to realise 'that providing people with basic services was limited to meeting immediate needs and did not tackle the root causes of poverty, which are found in the very unjust distribution of power and resources.' It works today with poor communities, helping them identify and demand their own rights.

Action Aid engages in research to further its aims.

AgBioIndia
http://www.agbioindia.org/
The AgBioIndia mailing list is an effort by the Forum for Biotechnology and Food Security 'to bridge the yawning gap in our understanding of the politics of food'. It is a non-commercial educational service for non-profit organisations and individuals. It aims to create wider awareness and understanding of the complexities of the crisis facing Indian agriculture and food security. In so doing it covers major developments in agriculture throughout the world.

Americas Program: A New World of Ideas, Analysis and Policy Options
http://www.americaspolicy.org/
This website is maintained by the Americas Program of the Interhemispheric Resource Center (IRC). Founded in 1979, the IRC is a small but dynamic non-profit policy studies centre whose overarching goal is to help forge a new global affairs agenda for the US government and people: one that makes the United States a more responsible global leader and partner.

It produces policy reports, issue briefs, political commentary, and popular education materials offering essential information and credible, forward-looking policy analysis.

ATTAC and ATTAC International
http://attac.org/indexen/index.html
ATTAC (Association pour la taxation des transactions financieres pour l'aide aux citoyens) was founded in France in 1998 and rapidly transformed into the International ATTAC (International movement for democratic control of financial markets and their institutions) at an international meeting in Paris, on 11–12 December 1998. It produces a weekly international newsletter, *Sand in the Wheels*.

Catholic Agency for Overseas Development (CAFOD)
http://www.cafod.org.uk/
CAFOD is a major British charity that has been fighting third world poverty since 1962. It is the English and Welsh arm of Caritas Internationalis, a worldwide network of Catholic relief and development organisations, working in partnership on over 1,000 programmes worldwide.

It raises money to finance long-term development work, emergency relief, analysis of the causes of under-development, campaigns on behalf of the world's poor, and education in England and Wales that raises aware-ness of the causes of third world poverty and promotes change.

The Center of Concern, USA
http://www.coc.org/
Through research, analysis, networking, public education and advocacy, the Center works to advance more just, sustainable and authentically human development for all, especially for the marginalized and those in poverty. It runs a Corporate Accountability Project; and a Food Secu-rity Project and has a web page of agribusiness links at http://www.coc.org/focus/private/agribusiness.html

CIDSE (Coopération internationale pour le developement et la solidarité – International Cooperation for Development and Solidarity)
http://www.cidse.org/en/
CIDSE is an international coalition of 15 Catholic devel-opment organisations, working together with organisa-tions and partners in the South and the North on development related issues. It is heavily involved in advocacy and lobbying work, and has task groups on the EU, trade and food security, social justice, and debt and structural adjustment.

Community Biodiversity Development and Conservation Programme (CBDC)
http://www.cbdcprogram.org
The CBDC is a global initiative developed by governmental and non-governmental organisations involved in agricultural initiatives in Africa, Asia and Latin America, in cooperation with 14 Northern partners, and is financed by four donor organisations: IDRC (Canada), Hivos (the Netherlands), SIDA (Sweden) and the Development Fund (Norway).

It aims to strengthen the ongoing work of farming communities in conserving and developing the agricultural biodiversity that is vital to their livelihood and food security.

Compassion in World Farming
http://www.ciwf.co.uk/
CWF campaigns to end the factory farming and long-distance transport of animals through hard-hitting political lobbying, investigations and high profile campaigns

It deals with such issues as banning live exports, the WTO and animal welfare, standards (e.g. the Little Red Tractor, the British Farm Standard trademark), broiler chickens and genetically modified animals.

Corporate Agri-business Research Project (CARP)
http://www.electricarrow.com/CARP/
The CARP was established to monitor corporate agribusiness from a public interest perspective through awareness, education, and action, while at the same time advocating the importance of building alternative, democratically controlled food systems. It seeks to serve family farmers, farm workers and consumers in their struggles for economic and social justice. It publishes a weekly e-mail newsletter *The Agri-business Examiner*.

The ETC Group: Action Group on Erosion, Technology and Concentration
478 River Avenue, Suite 200, Winnipeg, MB R3L 0C8 Canada
http://www.etcgroup.org/
Dedicated to the conservation and sustainable advancement of cultural and ecological diversity and human rights, the ETC group supports socially responsible developments of technologies useful to the poor and marginalised, and addresses international governance issues and corporate power. It concentrates on research and analysis of technological information (particularly but not exclusively plant genetic resources, biotechnologies and biological diversity), and in the development of strategic options related to the socioeconomic ramifications of new technologies. It works in partnership with civil society organizations for cooperative and sustainable self-reliance within disadvantaged societies, by providing information and analysis of socioeconomic and technological trends and alternatives. (Formerly known as RAFI – the Rural Advancement Foundation International.)

f3 – Foundation for Local Food Initiatives, UK
http://www.localfood.org.uk/
f3 is an independent not-for-profit cooperative company providing consultancy services to the local food sector. It aims to promote and support the growth of healthy local food economies as a key part of sustainable development. Sustainable local food systems need to be nurtured from the bottom up and f3 works closely with local, central and regional government, health, development agencies and community-based organisations to build local capacity.

Focus on the Global South
c/o CUSRI, Chulalongkorn University, Bangkok 10330, Thailand
http://focusweb.org/

[137]

Focus aims to consciously and consistently articulate, link and develop greater coherence between local community-based and national, regional and global paradigms of change. It strives to create a distinct and cogent link between development at the grassroots and the 'macro' levels. Particular emphasis on the Asia-Pacific region but nevertheless endeavours to both involve and closely network with those working on South issues elsewhere to share experiences, exchange ideas, and articulate sustainable alternatives and more just forms of regional and global governance.

It carries material by its director Walden Bellow, Aileen Kwa and others. Its *Focus on Trade* quarterly electronic bulletin contains some material on agriculture: http://www.focusweb.org/publications/Bulletins/Fot_index.htm

The Food Commission, UK
http://www.foodcomm.org.uk/
This is the UK's leading independent watchdog on food issues and has been campaigning for safer, healthier food since the late 1980s, exposing the poor practices and tricks of the food trade. Its campaigns have led the way towards improving food safety and standards. It publishes the *Food Magazine*.

Friends of the Earth, UK
http://www.foe.co.uk/campaigns/real_food/
The website provides resources tailored to the needs of a variety of groups, including campaigners, experts, farmers, general readers, local/regional decision makers, media, retailers, and under-16s. It deals with issues under the heads of food safety, threatened countryside, unfair trade and real food for all. It is particularly concerned with matters such as GMOs and farm trials, but also with other issues such as supermarkets and pesticide use.

Genetic Resources Action International (GRAIN)
http://www.grain.org/front/index.cfm
GRAIN is an international non-governmental organisation established in 1990 which promotes the sustainable management and use of agricultural biodiversity based on people's control over genetic resources and local knowledge. GRAIN works to protect and strengthen community control of agricultural biodiversity, to promote agriculture rich in biodiversity, and to stop the destruction of genetic diversity.

It publishes an excellent free quarterly magazine, *Seedling*.

Institute for Agriculture and Trade Policy (IATP)
2105 First Avenue South, Minneapolis, MN 55404–2505
http://www.iatp.org
The IATP promotes resilient family farms, rural communities and ecosystems around the world through research and education, science and technology, and advocacy.

It produces some of the finest analyses available on US and world agriculture today, for example by IATP members Mark Ritchie, Mark Muller, David Wallinga, Kristin Dawkins and Sophia Murphy. Much of their analysis is available free online, as is much else in the IATP document library. There are also links to related organisations .

In 1999, it opened WTO Watch in preparation for the WTO's Seattle ministerial meeting. As trade, globalisation and sustainable development issues have evolved since then, so has WTO Watch. In response to the growing interest in global trade policy, IATP has expanded its focus and merged WTO Watch with the Trade Observatory. This can be found at: http://www.tradeobservatory.org/pages/home.cfm

The Agri-business Center (http://www.agribusinesscenter.org/) is a new project of the IATP. It is a clearinghouse for information on agribusiness corporations.

International Federation of Organic Agriculture Movements (IFOAM)

IFOAM Head Office, c/o Ökozentrum Imsbach, D-66636 Tholey-Theley, Germany
http://www.ifoam.org/
IFOAM, founded in 1972, is the worldwide umbrella organisation of the organic agriculture movement, with about 750 member organisations and institutions in about 100 countries. Its main aims are to exchange knowledge and expertise among its members and to inform the public about organic agriculture; to represent, internationally, the organic movement in parliamentary, administrative and policy making forums (IFOAM has for example consultative status with the UNO and FAO); to set and regularly revise the international 'IFOAM Basic Standards of Organic Agriculture and Food Processing' (these IFOAM Basic Standards are translated into 19 languages); and to make an international guarantee of organic quality a reality.

International Society for Ecology and Culture (ISEC)

http://www.isec.org.uk/
ISEC is a non-profit organisation promoting locally based alternatives to the global consumer culture. It is concerned with the protection of both biological and cultural diversity. Its emphasis is on education for action: moving beyond single issues to look at the more fundamental influences that shape our lives. It has recently established an 'Ancient Futures Network' to bring together groups and individuals from every corner of the world that are struggling to maintain their cultural integrity in the face of economic globalisation.

ISEC's Local Food Programme aims to raise public awareness of issues of globalisation of the food economy in order to lay the foundations for community action and political change.

The Organization for Competitive Markets (OCM), US
http://www.competitivemarkets.com
OCM views the current consolidation of agriculture as a market failure resulting in misallocation of resources and the destruction of rural economies and culture. It is a multi-disciplinary non-profit group made up of farmers, ranchers, academics, attorneys, political leaders and business people. It provides research, information and advocacy towards a goal of increasing competition in the agricultural marketplace and protecting those markets from abuses of corporate power.

Pesticide Action Network UK (PAN UK)
http://www.pan-uk.org/
PAN UK promotes healthy food, agriculture and an environment which will provide food and meet public health needs without dependence on toxic chemicals, and without harm to food producers and agricultural workers. It is an independent, non-profit organisation. It works nationally and internationally with like-minded groups and individuals concerned with health, environment and development to eliminate the hazards of pesticides, reduce dependence on pesticides and prevent unnecessary expansion of their use, and increase the sustainable and ecological alternatives to chemical pest control.

Rural Futures, UK
http://www.ruralfutures.org
Rural Futures is a new countryside initiative by a number of organisations, between them representing millions of town and country people throughout Britain. It is a shared initiative between its stakeholders and is not a formal organisation in its own right

These stakeholders are: Friends of the Earth, the International Society for Ecology and Culture (ISEC), The Land is Ours, the National Trust, RSPB, the Small and Family Farms

Alliance, the Soil Association, the National Federation of Women's Institutes (NFWI), and National Federation of Young Farmers' Clubs.

> We have come together because there is a need to bring new thinking to the countryside debate. ... There is an urgent need to get to the roots of the difficulties facing rural communities and businesses throughout Britain. We need to explore and understand these, the real issues, without whose settlement there can be no prospect for a positive future for our countryside.

Soil Association, UK
http://www.soilassociation.org/
Founded in 1946, the Soil Association is the UK's leading campaigning and certification organisation for organic food and farming. It has developed organic standards and now works with consumers, farmers, growers, processors, retailers and policy makers. Its mission remains to create an informed body of public opinion and to promote organic agriculture as a sustainable alternative to intensive farming methods.

Sustain: the alliance for better food and farming, UK
http://www.sustainweb.org/index.asp
Sustain is a UK pressure group and network of more than 100 NGOs. It was launched in 1999 as a merger of the National Food Alliance and the Sustainable Agriculture Food and Environment (SAFE) Alliance, both of which had been established for over ten years. It advocates food and agriculture policies and practices that enhance the health and welfare of people and animals, improve the working and living environment, promote equity and enrich society and culture. Projects it runs include ones on food poverty, urban agriculture, and agriculture and trade, sustainable food chains, organic targets and food labelling.

Appendix 4: The CAP reform of 26 June 2003: last orders ...

On 26 June 2003, judging by what most commentators claimed, Europe took a decisive step towards a 'sustainable' agriculture; its citizens were going to enjoy nothing less than the end of productivist agriculture. A real 'revolution' was in the offing.

This almost unanimous media response was carefully orchestrated by the European Commission. It had two closely linked aims:

- To win over European consumers, who had become ever more demanding (but who nonetheless have a fairly weak understanding of the complex mechanics of agricultural policy), by convincing them that the reform was moving in the direction demanded by the wider society.
- To undermine the criticisms of those opposed to the reform, notably agricultural and development organisations, by rendering them inaudible or outmoded. If they were against a reform that is claimed to promote a sustainable agriculture, they could be portrayed as nothing but unreconstructed productivists, clinging out of pure self-interest to the advantages they have gained.

Alas, things are not as simply as the European Commission would have us believe. The Confederation of the Food and

Drink Industries of the EU, *the* organisation of agri-business in Europe, welcomed the reform the very next day as 'a major breakthrough for the agri-food sector [that]... will improve the EU's position in WTO negotiations'.[1] This was confirmed a few days later by the Director-General of the WTO, Supachai Panitchpakdi, who applauded that 'the EU has done a lot to advance the process' of WTO negotiations. He believed this would enable the WTO negotiators to make further progress in the agricultural arena and to get their teeth into liberalising other areas as well.[2]

There is no room for doubt. Agricultural policy was reformed in 2003 in the light of a further push for liberalisation of markets, and in such a way as to allow the EU to make important advances in the WTO negotiations in the area of services, for example, where it believes it has an unrivalled competitive edge.

Hearing this welcome from the foremost proponents of agri-business and free trade, who can still swallow unquestioningly the words of Franz Fischler, European Commissioner for Agriculture, waxing lyrical about the merits of a reform that will end 40 years of productivism in agriculture!

How can that be possible when the absence of any restraints on agricultural production or markets, in the USA following the reform of 2001 and now in the EU, is bound to depress production costs even further. Had the intention been to genuinely encourage farmers into quality production, it would have been necessary to allow them to increase their costs of production, rather than forcing these costs down. There are real costs to be met if you genuinely want to encourage quality and respect for the environment. Furthermore, the reform sets the existing distribution of subsidies among European farmers in stone; a totally unfair situation in which it is the largest and the most intensive farming units that generally receive the most substantial subsidies.

Finally, the reform only impinges on the margins in relation to the most industrialised areas of EU production: the breeding of pigs and poultry. As these areas are not in receipt of direct subsidies, producers here will not be affected by the social and environmental conditions attached to them. It is only the policies concerning animal welfare that will impact on them; everything suggests their effects will be marginal and that the largest producers will be able to make the minor adaptations needed, while small producers will not have the means to adapt. The gains for animal welfare overall will be negligible.

To have changed the model of agriculture it would have been necessary to change the basic assumptions, that is to say, the economic environment in which farming takes place. Sustainable agriculture just does not go with deregulation of markets.

I am grateful to Jean Damien Terreaux who provided material on the CAP reform at short notice long after the manuscript had been despatched.

Notes

Chapter 1

1. As Philip Lowe et al. put it in *Countryside Conflicts*:

   > The key to the Act [the Agriculture Act of 1957] lay in the idea that the annual price awards would never reimburse the farmer for all his [sic] costs of production. ...The farmer was required, in effect, to run up the down escalator; only if he could run faster than the escalator would he remain solvent or increase his profits. Caught in this cost-price squeeze, farmers had little option but to take up the grants on offer and to invest capital in new buildings, plant and machinery, to adopt new technologies, to make use of hitherto unproductive land, to remove any features that stood in the way of maximising production, to dispense with much of their labour force, and to concentrate production in larger units - in short to carry through the second industrial revolution. Those who did so prospered. Those who could not went under.

   Philip Lowe et al. (eds), *Countryside Conflict: The Politics of Farming, Forestry and Conservation*, Aldershot: Gower/Maurice Temple Smith, 1986, p. 43.

2. In the case of perishables such as fruit and vegetables where storage was not possible, they practised a simple withdrawal from the market, that is to say, the destruction of the produce concerned. This occurs in those sectors not protected by the CAP in the same way as the basic producers, notably of cereals, that are left to the free play of the market.

3. SCPs are mainly fabricated using a base of by-products of the agri-food industry, notably corn gluten feed, citrus pellets and the like. Manioc also counts among the SCPs.

4. The full Compassion in World Farming analysis of WTO rules from an animal welfare perspective will be found at

http://www.worldtradecruelty.com/frameset-report.htm

5. Ibid.

6. As shown in the agricultural census, *Récensement générale de l'agriculture, 1970–71.*

7. Madeleine Lefrançois, *La Chasse aux paysans*, Paris: Stock, 1976.

8. Jacques Berthelot, *L'agriculture, talon d'achille de la mondialisation*, Paris: L'Harmattan, 2001, ch 3, pp.68–89.

9. Jacques Berthelot, *L'agriculture*, p. 70.

10. See Sophia Murphy's *Managing the Invisible Hand: Markets, Farmers and International Trade*, IATP, April 2002 for an excellent analysis of the role of transnationals. Text available at www.wtowatch.org/library/admin/uploadedfiles/Managing_the_Invisible_Hand_2.pdf

11. Thanks to Jacques Berthelot for supplying this box.

12. Maurice Doyon, Daniel-M Gouin and Nicolas Paillat, *Critical Analysis of the Concept of the Producer Subsidy Equivalent in the Dairy Sector (Dairy PSE)*, GREPA, Université Laval, Québec, 13 November 2001.

13. *Milking the CAP*, Oxfam briefing paper No. 34, December 2002, http://www.oxfam.org.uk/policy/papers/34milking/34milking.html

14. 26 June 2003, http://www.cafod.org.uk/tradejustice/cap20030625.shtml

15. AGRA Presse Hebdo, 30 March 2001.

16. Jacques Berthelot, *L'agriculture*.

17. EU Commission, *Agriculture in the European Union: Statistical and Economic Information 2001*, February 2002.

Chapter 2

1. Com (91) 100 final, *The Development and Future of the CAP*, Reflections Paper of the Commission, p. 3.

2. Eutrophication is a condition in an aquatic ecosystem where high nutrient concentrations stimulate blooms of algae (e.g. phytoplankton).

3. www.defra.gov.uk/environment/water/quality/nitrate/intro.htm

4. Material for the original edition supplied by Philippe Pointereau.

5. OFIVAL (Office interprofessionel des viandes) website www.ofival.fr/coataions/indexcot.htm

6. John Madeley, 'Trade and Hunger: An Overview of Case Studies on the Impact of Trade Liberalisation on Food Security', *Globala Studier*, no. 4, October 2000. A report from Church of Sweden Aid, Diakonia, Forum Syd, the Swedish Society for Nature Conservation and the Programme of Global Studies.

7. As Jacques Berthelot has chronicled extensively, see Jacques Berthelot, *L'agriculture*, Part 3, 'Putting Internal Supports into Boxes and how it

is Camouflaged by the US and the EU', pp. 215–91.

8. See *Agenda 2000* at www.europa.eu.int/comm/agenda2000/index_en.htm and *Reform of the Common Agricultural Policy (CAP)* at www.europa.eu.int/scadplus/leg/en/lvb/l60002.htm for details of the proposals for agriculture.

9. Rural development becomes the second pillar of the CAP. For the first time, the foundations have been laid for a comprehensive and consistent rural development policy whose task will be to supplement market management by ensuring that agricultural expenditure is devoted more than in the past to spatial development and nature conservancy, the establishment of young farmers, etc.

(Reform of the CommonAagricultural Policy (CAP))

10. As part of the cannibalistic merry-go-round that is an economically essential part of the meat industry, all the bits of animals from slaughterhouses unsuitable for human consumption are boiled up to produce fat and protein. The protein makes animal feed. Apart from the obvious high risk of different infections being passed on, it seems strange that nobody had actually questioned the biological sense of forcing naturally vegetarian animals to become carnivores, eating the remains of other animals. This is probably what has caused the spread of BSE.

(Professor Richard Lacey, *How Now Mad Cow?*
www.mad-cow.org/lacey.html)

11. Press release, Brussels, 26 February 2001:

The European Union today approved the European Commission's groundbreaking proposal to eliminate quotas and duties on all products except arms from the world's 48 poorest countries. The EU Council of Ministers, meeting in Brussels, agreed to the plan, which will make the EU the world's first major trading power to commit itself to opening its market fully to the world's poorest countries. Welcoming the move, European Trade Commissioner Pascal Lamy told a press conference: 'It's a worldwide first. At the end of the day, we will have 100 per cent access, with no exclusions, except of course for arms. We have delivered on our fine words. This sends a signal to the rest of the world that we are serious about getting the most disadvantaged to share in the fruits of trade liberalisation.' Mr Lamy paid tribute to United Nations Secretary-General Kofi Annan, who had personally written to EU Heads of State to encourage them to support the measure. Swedish Trade Minister Lief Pagrotsky, who chaired the meeting of EU ministers, said: 'We hope this will put pressure on other countries to follow our example.'

12. *Sand in the Wheels* is the name of ATTAC's weekly English-language newsletter.

Chapter 3

1. Paol Gorneg, 'Voyage au Coeur de la FNSEA', *Le Monde diplomatique*, no. 562, January 2001.
2. Ibid.
3. Gordon Wright, *Rural Revolution in France: The Peasantry in the Twentieth Century,* Stanford, Stanford University Press, 1964, pp. 121–22.
4. Muriel Gremillet et Frédéric Pons, 'Fissures dans l'agricole', *Libération*, 31 January 2001.
5. See Gordon Wright, *Rural Revolution in France*, p. 170.

Chapter 4

1. Réseau des organisations paysannes et des producteurs de l'Afrique de l'ouest (West African Network of Small Farmer and Producer Organisations).
2. http://www.sosfaim.be/docs/com_presse_roppa_vc.pdf
3. Lamy, speech in Sydney, 17 July 2002: www.ecdel.org.au/pressandinformation/Speech_Lamy_EABC.htm
4. Five out of the 11 agreements with Mediterranean countries have already been concluded, that with Tunisia being for the moment the only one which includes an agricultural section.
5. Gérard Surdez, 'Contribution à la réflexion sur le partenariat euro-méditerranéen': www.attac.org/euromed/documents/contrib_surdez.rtf
6. National Farmers Union, NFU News, April 1999. On the web at http://www.nfu.org/index.cfm?category=newsroom&category2=nf unews&category3=x&category4=x&category5=x
7. Janette Habel, 'Vers le plus grand espace économique du monde. Intégration à marche forcée pour les Ameriques', *Le Monde diplomatique*, October 2000, pp. 12-13.
8. Preface to Dr. Alejandro Nadal, *The Environmental and Social Impacts of Economic Liberalization on Corn Production in Mexico*, Oxfam GB and WWF International, Sept 2000. This section is largely based on this report.
9. *Globalisation and Liberalisation: Implications for Poverty, Distribution and Inequality*, UNDP Occasional Paper 32. 1997.
10. Frank Ackerman, 'Is the United States a Pollution Haven?', IATP, press release, 4 March 2002, (via iatp@iatp.org).
11. http://www.citizen.org/documents/ACFF2.PDF

12. Horacio Martins de Carvalho, 'Democratização econômica e social no campo', in Senador Geraldo Cándido, *Situação e perspectives da agriculture brasileira*, Brasilia, Senado, 2000.

13. 'IFAD Strategy for Rural Poverty Reduction in Latin America and the Caribbean, March 2002, www.ifad.org/operations/regional/2002/pl/pl.htm

   IFAD is a specialised agency of the United Nations, established as an international financial institution in 1977 as one of the major outcomes of the 1974 World Food Conference, itself a response to the Sahelian food crises in Africa in the early 1970s.

14. 'IFAD Strategy for Rural Poverty Reduction in Latin America and the Caribbean, March 2002, www.ifad.org/operations/regional/2002/pl/pl.htm

15. 'Experience with the implementation of the Uruguay Round', Agreement on Agriculture: developing country experiences (based on case studies), FAO Symposium on Agriculture, Trade and Food Security, , Geneva, 23-24 September 1999 at
   http://www.fao.org/docrep/meeting/x3065e.htm

Chapter 5

1. COPA, Comité des organisations professionnelles agricoles de l'Union Européenne, is the European Union wide farmers' organisation; COGECA, Comité générale de la coopération agricole de l'Union Européenne, is the EU federation of agricultural cooperatives.

2. Compassion in World Farming has said of the Little Red Tractor that it is a 'cynical attempt to make a marketing virtue out of meeting the bare legal minimum', allowing intensive chicken breeding, the use of narrow farrowing crates for breeding pigs and of battery cages for laying hens, and animal mutilations such as the debeaking of chickens and the tail docking of pigs.

   See www.redtractortruth.com/

3. Conclusions of the Agriculture Council on 20 and 21 November 2000: WTO Negotiations on Agriculture - EC Comprehensive Negotiating Proposal, europa.eu.int/comm/agriculture/external/wto/document/neg_en.pdf

4. Press release, Franz Fischler in Berlin,
   europa.eu.int/rapid/start/cgi/guesten.ksh?p_action.gettxt=gt&doc=IP/02/1125|0|RAPID&lg=EN&display=

5. No one campaigning for reform of the CAP in the interests of citizens or of small farmers has a good word to say for this reform, despite the welcome it has been given in the world¹s media. See, for example, Oxfam's press release 'EEU CAP Reforms a Disaster for the Poor',

http://www.maketradefair.com/stylesheet.asp?file=27062003112201

6. The US government does not pretend that all its farm subsidies are decoupled – notably its marketing loan payments and the new counter-cyclical payments – but rather that they remain within the authorised limits for 'coupled' or 'amber box' subsidies, largely because it cheats in two ways in its notifications of domestic subsidies to the WTO, by:

   1) putting some of them in the 'non specific' AMS (or amber box) subsidies, which are exempted from reduction by the *de minimis* provision as long as they remain under 5 per cent of the agricultural production value, i.e. more or less under $10 billion; and
   2) putting other subsidies into the 'green box' of authorised subsidies which are clearly 'coupled' to production and should have been put in the amber box.
      'Of course,' remarks Jacques Berthelot, 'the EU cheats on a comparable scale...' (Berthelot, *L'Agriculture*)

7. See the April 2003 IATP report on dumping (summary at www.tradeobservatory.org/FAQ/faq.cfm?faq_id=8#757)

Chapter 6

1. In France, for instance, there are five large wholesalers and a few dozen agri-food transnationals who stand between 300,000 French farmers and 60 million consumers. This is even more true in times of crisis and the more distribution is integrated with production (as is the case with the pork, poultry and fish).
2. François de Ravignan, *Actes du 1er Congrès national de l'installation progressive*, Nîmes, 1999.
3. de Ravignan, *Actes du 1er Congrès national*.
4. cf. P.Pavie, 'Concentration à tout bout de champ', *Campagnes solidaires*, no. 155, September 2001.

Appendix 4

1. Press release at www.ciaa.be/uk/documents/press/press26-06-03.htm
2. *Financial Times*, French edition (*Courrier International*, 10–16 juillet 2003).

Index